C000147884

ROCK & ROLL

Facts, Figures & Fun

"Any book without a mistake in it has had
too much money spent on it"
Sir William Collins, publisher

ROCK & ROLL

Facts, Figures & Fun

MIKE EVANS

ff&f

Rock & Roll
Facts, Figures & Fun

Published by
Facts, Figures & Fun, an imprint of
AAPPL Artists' and Photographers' Press Ltd.
10 Hillside, London SW19 4NH, UK
info@ffnf.co.uk www.ffnf.co.uk
info@aappl.com www.aappl.com

Sales and Distribution
UK and export: Turnaround Publisher Services Ltd.
orders@turnaround-uk.com
USA and Canada: Sterling Publishing Inc. sales@sterlingpub.com
Australia & New Zealand: Peribo Pty. peribomec@bigpond.com
South Africa: Trinity Books. trinity@iafrica.com

Copyright © AAPPL Artists' and Photographers' Press Ltd 2006

All rights reserved. No part of this publication may be
reproduced, stored in a retrieval system, copied, or transmitted
in any form or by any means, electronic, mechanical,
photocopying, recording or otherwise without the prior
written permission of the copyright owner.

A catalogue record for this book is available from the
British Library.

ISBN 13: 9781904332367
ISBN 10: 1904332366

Design (contents and cover): Malcolm Couch
mal.couch@blueyonder.co.uk

Printed in China by Imago Publishing
info@imago.co.uk

For information about custom editions, special sales, premium
and corporate purchases, please contact ffnf Special Sales
+44 20 8971 2094 or info@ffnf.co.uk

Contents

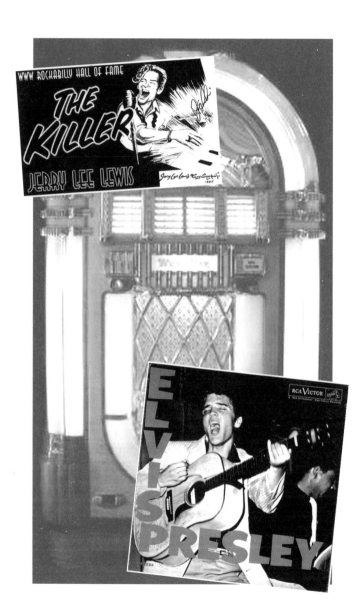

THE ROOTS OF ROCK'N'ROLL

THE NAME

The phrase "rock and roll" crops up in a number of old blues songs as a slang reference to the sexual act. As early as 1922 blues singer Trixie Smith recorded a song called 'My Daddy Rocks Me (With One Steady Roll)'. And in 1934, the jazz-tinged vocal trio The Boswell Sisters sang 'Rock and Roll' in a now-forgotten movie starring Jack Benny, *Transatlantic Merry-Go-Round*.

A rhythm and blues song entitled 'Rock and Roll' was released in 1949 by boxing champ-turned-saxophone star Wild Bill Moore.

The term was first used as a generic name by Cleveland DJ Alan Freed in 1952, when he launched his nightly *Moondog Rock'n'Roll Show* playing black rhythm and blues discs to an audience of mainly white teenagers.

The term "rhythm and blues" was itself coined by legendary producer-to-be Jerry Wexler in 1947, then working for *Billboard* magazine. The previous "race records" was considered demeaning, and on June 17, 1949 the term was first used for the magazine's "race" charts.

The first major hit single to have "rock and roll" in its title wasn't actually a rock record, but an early cash-in on the new craze by ex-Glenn Miller vocalist Kay Starr. Released in January 1956, 'Rock And Roll Waltz' topped the charts on both sides of the Atlantic.

"Rock'n'Roll" first appeared in a hit album title with *Rock'n'Roll Stage Show* by Bill Haley and his Comets in 1956. In Britain the long-player made it to number 30 on the singles chart, the first LP lists not being compiled until 1958.

SOME PRE-ROCK'N'ROLL "ROCK" RECORDS

1947	Good Rockin' Tonight	Roy Brown
1948	We're Gonna Rock	Wild Bill Moore
1948	Rockin' The House	Memphis Slim
1949	Rockin' At Midnight	Roy Brown
1949	Rock The House	Tiny Grimes
1949	Rock The Joint	Jimmy Preston
1949	Rock and Roll	Wild Bill Moore
1950	Rockin' The Blues	Pee Wee Crayton
1950	Rock With It	Johnny Moore's Three Blazers
1950	I'm Gonna Rock	Connie Jordan
1950	Rockin' Blues	Johnny Otis
1951	Rockin' and Rollin'	Little Son Jackson

"If anyone asks you what kind of music you play, tell him 'pop'.
Don't tell him 'rock'n'roll' or they won't even let you in the hotel"
Buddy Holly

ORIGINS

The roots of rock'n'roll are to be found in blues, rhythm and blues, country and even gospel music. The synthesis that made it possible came about via pioneering US record labels in the early 1950s, the most important of which were Sun Records in Memphis, Atlantic in New York City and Chicago's Chess label.

Rock's roots in the blues were personified in the roster of Chess Records. Founded by brothers Phil and Leonard Chess in 1949, the Chicago label – and its subsidiary Checker – featured southern blues names including Elmore James, Sonny Boy Williamson, Little Walter and, most significantly, Muddy Waters. These and others typified an electric big-city version of country blues which directly influenced Chess's biggest rock'n'roll names Bo Diddley and Chuck Berry, and a few years later English R&B bands like the Rolling Stones.

CHESS IN THE R&B CHARTS

Chess and Checker artists made regular appearances at the top of the US rhythm and blues charts during the early 1950s.

1951	Jackie Brenston	Rocket 88	#1
1952	Howlin' Wolf	How Many More Years	#4
1952	Little Walter	Juke	#1
1952	Willie Mabon	I Don't Know	#1
1953	Willie Mabon	I'm Mad	#1
1954	Muddy Waters	Hoochie Coochie Man	#3
1955	Little Walter	My Babe	#1

In Memphis, Sam Phillips' Sun Records also started as a blues-based label with R&B artists that included Rufus Thomas, Little

Junior Parker and Ike Turner. But Phillips also recorded local country-based artists – "hillbilly" they were called in those days – like Harmonica Frank, Charlie Feathers and The Starlite Wranglers. And Sun also pioneered a new breed of rockers who combined both traditions, in what became known as rockabilly. This was the ground-breaking rock'n'roll epitomized by Carl Perkins, Billy "The Kid" Emerson and the young Elvis Presley. Phillips sold Elvis' contract to RCA for $35,000 in November 1955, and the rest, as they say, is history.

SUN ROCKABILLIES
Rockabilly hits on the Sun label included these timeless classics.

1955	Mystery Train	Elvis Presley	C&W chart#1
1956	Blue Suede Shoes	Carl Perkins	Pop chart #2
1956	Ooby Doobie	Roy Orbison	Pop chart #59
1957	Whole Lotta Shakin Goin' On	Jerry Lee Lewis	Pop chart #3
1957	Great Balls of Fire	Jerry Lee Lewis	Pop chart #2

As early as 1942 Capitol Records had their first hit with a country-swing crossover, 'Cow-Cow Boogie' by Ella Mae Morse and boogie pianist Freddie Slack. Dubbed "Western Swing", the mix of cowboy music and blues was another precursor to rock'n'roll, and leading lights of the genre included Bob Wills and his Texas Playboys, Merrill Moore, and Bill Haley & the Saddlemen.

As well as heralding rock'n'roll with a pile of R&B hits that included Joe Turner's 1954 classic 'Shake Rattle and Roll' (later successfully covered by both Bill Haley and Elvis Presley), Atlantic Records was also a cornerstone for the rock'n'roll vocal group style known as doo-wop. The label (founded by Ahmet and Nesuhi Ertegun) nurtured groups like the Clovers, the Drifters and The Coasters, all of whom had their background in the gospel music of Black America. It also laid the foundations for soul music with the gospel-tinged R&B of Ray Charles – whose first album on the label in 1957, *Ray Charles*, was sub-titled *Rock & Roll*.

Doo-Wop evolved on the street corners of New York and other American cities, where unaccompanied vocal outfits would rehearse their "shoo-wop, doo-wah" phrases – hence the name. Mainly from the black and Italian-American ghettos, the earliest doo-woppers adopted "bird" names – The Orioles, The Ravens and The Crows, soon followed by The Robins, The Penguins, The Flamingos, The Falcons and many more.

THE ORIGINAL ROCK'N'ROLL RECORD

There have been several contenders for what fans and critics consider the first-ever true rock'n'roll record. Fats Domino's 'The Fat Man' of 1949 has often been suggested, as has Bill Haley's 'Rock The Joint' released in 1953. But by general consensus the honour falls to 'Rocket '88'', recorded by Jackie Brenston and his Delta Cats in 1951. The band were actually Ike Turner's Kings of Rhythm, but when the outfit came to record two singles at the Memphis Recording Service, producer Sam Phillips credited the numbers that saxophonist Brenston sang to him. Phillips, who had still to form Sun Records, leased the discs to Chess in Chicago.

The title came from the eight-cylinder Oldsmobile 88, reckoned to be the fastest saloon on the road in '51 – magazine ads for the car even pictured a man and woman astride a space rocket.

The single features an ahead-of-its time distorted guitar sound that was achieved accidentally when Phillips stuffed a damaged amplifier speaker with paper; the fracture having occurred when the amp fell off the roof of the band's car on Highway 61 as they sped to the session from Clarksdale, Mississippi. And with its booting saxophones and some frantic vocals, it sounded like nothing that had gone before.

When it hit No1 on the R&B charts, 'Rocket '88" convinced Phillips of the value in starting his own record label, which resulted in Sun Records the following year. And it heralded a new, wilder take on R&B which would soon be called "rock'n'roll."

Rocket '88'
Jackie Brenston and his Delta Cats
Chess / #1458

B-side: Come Back Where You Belong
Released: April 1951

Composer: Jackie Brenston
Recorded: Memphis Recording Service, March 1951
Producer: Sam Phillips
Personnel: Jackie Brenston (vocals),
Ike Turner (piano), Wille Kizart (guitar),
Raymond Hill, Eugene Fox (saxophones),
Jesse Knight Jnr (bass),
Willie Sims (drums)

"Rock's so good to me. Rock is my child and my grandfather"
Chuck Berry

THE PIONEERS

Although Elvis Presley is often credited as having ignited the rock'n'roll explosion in the mid-50s, several rock artists had discs in the charts before "the Pelvis" hit the #1 spot with 'Heartbreak Hotel' in the early months of 1956. They included Fats Domino, Little Richard and – most significantly – Bill Haley and his Comets.

Profile: BILL HALEY

Born: William John Clifton Haley, 6 July 1925, Detroit, Michigan.

Died: 9 February 1981, Harlingen, Texas.

Chart Debut: Dim Dim The Lights [US#11, 1954], Shake Rattle And Roll [UK#4, 1954]

Major Hits: Dim Dim The Lights, Shake Rattle And Roll [1954], Mambo Rock, Rock Around The Clock, Rock-A-Beatin' Boogie, Birth Of The Boogie, Burn That Candle, Razzle Dazzle [1955], See You Later Alligator, The Saints Rock'n'Roll, Rip It Up, Rudy's Rock, R-O-C-K, Rockin' Through The Rye [1956], Don't Knock The Rock [1957]

Facts'n'Figures: 'Rock Around The Clock' is one of the biggest selling singles of all time, having sold an estimated thirty million copies. It hit the charts four times, and was featured in the movies *Blackboard Jungle* [1955], *Rock Around The Clock* [1956] and *American Graffiti* [1974]

Bill Haley and his Comets recorded 'Rock Around The Clock' as a B-side for their first Decca Records recording session. The A-side was a song called 'Thirteen Women And Only One Man In Town'.

Through 1955 and 1956, Haley had more chart entries in the UK than in the USA. When he visited Britain early in 1957 – as the first major American rock'n'roll act to tour the country – there were unprecedented scenes from the moment he set foot at London's Waterloo Station, after a train chartered by the *Daily Mirror* newspaper had brought him, the Comets and several hundred prize-winner fans from the port of Southampton. The mayhem at the station was dubbed by the press as the "Second Battle of Waterloo"!

Profile: FATS DOMINO

Born: Antoine Domino, 26 February 1928, New
　　　Orleans, Louisiana

Chart Debut: Ain't That A Shame [US#10, 1955]

Major Hits: Ain't That A Shame [1955], I'm In Love
　　　Again, Blueberry Hill, My Blue Heaven, When My
　　　Dreamboat Comes Home [1956], Blue Monday, I'm
　　　Walkin', Valley Of Tears, It's You I Love [1957], Whole
　　　Lotta Loving [1958], I Want To Walk You Home, Be
　　　My Guest [1959], Walkin' To New Orleans [1960].

Facts 'n Figures: Fats' debut single 'The Fat Man', released in 1949, sold over a million by 1953. Between 1955 and 1963 he had 37 entries in the US Top Forty, 20 of them also charting in the UK.

Rhythm and blues man Fats Domino first hit the rock'n'roll scene in 1955 when 'Ain't That A Shame,' was covered by the clean-cut white crooner Pat Boone. Boone's version went to number one, the first of many hits. Other watered-down covers of rock'n'roll and R&B songs by Boone included Little Richard's 'Tutti Frutti' and 'Long Tall Sally', and Ivory Joe Hunter's 'I Almost Lost My Mind.' Pioneer DJ Alan Freed, promoting black R&B to white audiences, even refused to play any Boone records on his radio shows.

Profile: LITTLE RICHARD

Born: Richard Wayne Penniman, 5 December 1932, Macon, Georgia

Chart Debut: Tutti Frutti [US#17, 1956]

Major Hits: Tutti Frutti, Rip It Up, Long Tall Sally, Slippin' And Slidin' [1956], She's Got It, The Girl Can't Help It, Lucille, Jenny Jenny, Keep A Knockin' [1957], Good Golly Miss Molly [1958], Baby Face, By The Light Of The Silvery Moon [1959].

Facts'n'Figures: Little Richard sold over 18 million records by the end of the Fifties and appeared in three early rock'n'roll films *Don't Knock The Rock* [1956], *Mister Rock'n'Roll* [1957] and the classic *The Girl Can't Help It* [1956]

Little Richard's "Awop-bop-a-loo-mop-alop-bam-boom" intro to 'Tutti Frutti' remains the most celebrated opening line in rock'n'roll.

Profile: ELVIS PRESLEY

Born: Elvis Aaron Presley, 8 January 1935, Tupelo, Mississippi.

Died: 16 August 1977, Memphis, Tennessee.

Chart Debut: Heartbreak Hotel [US#1, UK#2, 1956]

Major 'Fifties Hits: Heartbreak Hotel, Blue Suede Shoes, I Want You I Need You I Love You, Hound Dog/ Don't Be Cruel, Love Me Tender, Love Me, Blue Moon [1956], Too Much, All Shook Up, Teddy Bear, Loving You, Paralysed, Party, Jailhouse Rock, Santa Bring My Baby Back To Me [1957], Don't, I Beg Of You, Wear My Ring Around Your Neck, Hard Headed Woman, King Creole, One Night, I Got Stung [1958], A Fool Such As I, I Need Your Love Tonight, A Big Hunk O' Love [1959]

Facts'n'Figures: The double-sided smash 'Hound Dog' / 'Don't Be Cruel' was the most popular 2-sided hit in history. With both showing equally strongly in the US chart, *Billboard* alternated the titles through the record's 11-week run at #1. It went on to sell nearly ten million worldwide.

Through 1956 Elvis had 10 singles, nine EPs and two albums released by RCA. His debut album *Elvis Presley* stayed at #1 in the US LP chart for ten weeks and in the Top 40 for 48 weeks – just less than a year. It was RCA's first long-player to sell over a million. And in August 1956 RCA made history by releasing seven Elvis singles on the same day!

Elvis was the first of the rock'n'roll big spenders. As soon as he made it big, he had a habit of buying cars – usually top-of-the-range Cadillacs – for all and sundry. Legend has it he once walked into a Memphis car showroom and there and then bought a flash Caddy for the lady cleaning the floor.

When Elvis Presley was inducted into the US Army on 24th March 1958, the American government started losing an estimated $500,000 in lost taxes for each year that he served.

SKIFFLE MANIA

Britain's contribution to the early development of rock'n'roll came in the unlikely form of the skiffle boom. When Lonnie Donegan hit the US and UK Top Ten with 'Rock Island Line' early in 1956, it triggered a craze for do-it-yourself groups among British teenagers. With guitars, home-made tea-chest basses and washboards, thousands of skifflers banged out the Donegan-inspired repertoire of American blues and folk songs, leaning heavily on the work of Woody Guthrie, Leadbelly and such.

As well as providing Donegan with over twenty chart hits over the next five years, skiffle introduced a generation of UK teenagers to some of the real roots of rock'n'roll. And equally importantly, it put guitars in the hands of schoolboy would-be rockers including The Beatles, Eric Clapton, The Rolling Stones and many more.

Profile: LONNIE DONEGAN
Born: Anthony Donegan, 29 April 1931, Glasgow, Scotland.
Died: 3 November 2002, Peterborough, England.
Chart Debut: Rock Island Line [US#8, UK#8, 1956]
Major Hits: Rock Island Line, Lost John, Bring A Little Water Sylvie/ Dead Or Alive [1956], Don't You Rock Me Daddy-O, Cumberland Gap, Gamblin' Man/ Putting On The Style [1957], Grand Coolie Dam, Tom Dooley [1958]; Does Your Chewing Gum Lose Its Flavour, The Battle Of New Orleans [1959], My Old Man's A Dustman [1960]

LAUREATES OF ROCK: LEIBER & STOLLER

The greatest songwriting team in early rock'n'roll, Jerry Leiber (born 25 April 1933, Baltimore Maryland) and Mike Stoller (born 13 May 1933, Belle Harbor, NY) met in Los Angeles where their parents had moved after World War II. They started writing songs in the early Fifties for rhythm and blues artists such as Amos Milburn and Jimmy Witherspoon, having their first national R&B hit in 1952 with 'Hard Times', recorded by Charles Brown. The same year the duo had their first major success with Big Mama Thornton and 'Hound Dog', which in 1956 became a marathon hit for Elvis Presley.

After forming the Spark label in 1954 they signed LA vocal group the Robins, who became the Coasters when Leiber and Stoller moved to New York as independent producers for Atlantic Records. A string of humourous "playlets" for the group, all penned and produced by the two songwriters, included such classic as 'Riot In Cell Block # 9' (1954),

'Smokey Joe's Café' (1955) 'Searchin'' (1957) and their biggest, 'Yakety Yak' in 1958.

Writing hits for other Atlantic stars like LaVerne Baker and Ruth Brown, the pair hit paydirt yet again for the label with a series of masterpieces with the Drifters, songs like 'There Goes My Baby' (1959), 'Save The Last Dance For Me' (1960) and 'Up On The Roof' which became part of the musical fabric of the era. And when the Drifters' lead singer Ben E King went solo, they contnued to furnish him with huge hits. Outside of their Atlantic work they also famously penned hits for Elvis Presley, including 'Jailhouse Rock' (1957) and 'King Creole' (1958).

Through the first half of the Sixties they became closely associated with the Brill Building 'song factory', acting as mentors to Phil Spector before setting up the Red Bird and Blue Cat labels in 1964. Classics on the labels included the hits of the Shangri Las ('Remember (Walkin' In The Sand) and 'Leader Of The Pack') and 'Chapel Of Love' by the Dixie Cups.

Into the Seventies Leiber and Stoller continued producing on a freelance basis with artists such as Elkie Brooks ('Pearl's A Singer', 1976), Procul Harum and Stealers Wheel (1973's classic 'Stuck In The Middle With You'), but it was as seminal songwriters in the Fifties and early Sixties that they made their biggest mark on the rock'n'roll landscape.

SIX OF LEIBER & STOLLER'S BIGGEST

1957	Elvis Presley	Jailhouse Rock	US#1, UK#1
1958	Elvis Presley	King Creole	UK#2
1958	Coasters	Yakety Yak	US#1
1959	Drifters	There Goes My Baby	US#2
1960	Drifters	Save The Last Dance For Me	US#1, UK#2
1961	Ben E King	Stand By Me	US#4, UK#1

═══ CLASSIC ROCK'N'ROLL ═══

In the wake of the rock'n'roll revolution spearheaded by Haley, Domino, Richard and Elvis, the second half of the Fifties saw a wealth of important singles by now-legendary performers, solid-gold classics that have stood the test of time and influenced generations of musicians and vocalists ever since. Here are some of the best.

Chuck Berry/ Sweet Little Sixteen [US#2, 1958]
Rock's first poet with the definitive paen to the eternal teenage fan.

The Coasters/ Yaketty Yak [US#1, 1958]
An anthem for put-upon kids everywhere, and the Coasters' biggest hit.

Eddie Cochran/ Summertime Blues [US#8, 1958]
Cochran was one of 50s rock's real figures of rebellion, and a fine guitar player.

Danny and the Juniors/ At The Hop [US#1, 1957]
A now- nostalgic single that has far outlasted the group who performed it.

Bobby Darin/ Splish Splash [US#3, 1958]
Darin recorded some fine rock'n'roll sides before developing as a "straight" crooner aiming at the mainstream market.

Dell-Vikings/ Come Go With Me   [US#4, 1957]
One of the great doo-wop records, the lyrics minimal but to maximum vocal effect.

Everly Brothers/ Wake Up Little Suzie [US#1, 1957]
The Everly Brothers' hits were country rock ahead of its time.

Buddy Holly & the Crickets/ That'll Be The Day [US#1, 1957]
A pop anthem confirming that, despite a slightly nurdish image, Holly was a tough rock'n'roller at heart.

Jerry Lee Lewis/ Great Balls Of Fire [US#2, 1957]
A pumping piano thumper in the midst of rockabilly guitarists, wild man Jerry Lee was one of the greatest graduates of Sun Records.

Frankie Lymon and the Teenagers/ Why Do Fools Fall In Love [US#6, 1956]
Pint-sized Lymon was only thirteen when he made *the* teenybop anthem of its day.

Johnny Otis/ Willie and the Hand Jive [US#9, 1958]
Otis' ode to the dance you could do sitting down pioneered the shuffle beat later attributed to Bo Diddley.

Carl Perkins/ Blue Suede Shoes [US#2, 1956]
Though former Sun label mate Elvis covered it more successfully, Perkins' original retains the raw power of pure rockabilly.

Gene Vincent/ Be Bop A Lula [US#7, 1956]
Heavy on echo and attitude, the archetypal "rebel rocker" disc.

Larry Williams/ Slow Down [1958]
The Beatles covered several of Williams' songs including this masterpiece and its flipside 'Dizzy Miss Lizzy.'

Paul Anka's 1957 worldwide smash 'Diana' sold over nine million copies. He'd written the song when 15 as a poem for the family's 18-year-old babysitter, then later set it to music. It was released just four months after he won a trip to New York by collecting soup tin labels, where he was signed to a record deal at the age of 16.

ROCK'N'ROLL PROFILES

CHUCK BERRY

Born: Charles Edward Anderson Berry, 18
   October 1926, San Jose, California.

Chart Debut: Maybelline [US#5, 1955]

Major Hits: Maybelline [1955], School Days, Rock
   & Roll Music [1957], Sweet Little Sixteen,
   Johnny B. Goode [1958], No Particular Place To
   Go [1964], My Ding-A-Ling [1972]

EDDIE COCHRAN

Born: Edward Ray Cochrane, 3 October 1938,
   Oklahoma City, Oklahoma.

Died: 17 April 1960, nr. Bath, England.

Chart Debut: Sittin' In The Balcony [US#18,
   1957]

Major Hits: Sittin' In The Balcony, Summertime
   Blues [1958], C'mon Everybody [1959], Three
   Steps To Heaven [1960]

EVERLY BROTHERS

Born: Isaac Donald (Don) Everly, 1 February 1937,
   Brownie, Kentucky. Phillip (Phil) Everly, 19
   January 1939, Chicago, Illinois.

Chart Debut: Bye Bye Love [US#2, 1957]

Major Hits: Bye Bye Love, Wake Up Little Susie
   [1957], All I Have To Do Is Dream, Bird Dog,
   Problems [1958], ('Til) I Kissed You [1959], Let
   It Be Me, Cathy's Clown, When Will I Be Loved,
   Lucille [1960], Walk Right Back, Ebony Eyes,
   Temptation [1961], Cryin' In The Rain, That's
   Old Fashioned [1962], The Price Of Love
   [1965].

BUDDY HOLLY
Born: Charles Hardin Holley, 7 September 1936, Lubbock, Texas.
Died: 3 February 1959, nr. Mason City, Iowa.
Chart Debut: That'll Be The Day [US#1, UK#1, 1957]
Major Hits: That'll Be The Day, Peggy Sue, Oh Boy! [1957], Maybe Baby, Rave On, [1958], It Doesn't Matter Anymore [1959]

JERRY LEE LEWIS
Born: 29 September 1935, Ferriday, Louisiana.
Chart Debut: Whole Lotta Shakin' Going On [US#3, 1957]
Major Hits: Whole Lotta Shakin' Going On, Great Balls Of Fire [1957], Breathless, High School Confidntial [1958]

GENE VINCENT
Born: Vincent Eugene Craddock, 11 February 1935, Norfolk, Virginia.
Died: 12 October 1971, Newhall, California.
Chart Debut: Be-Bop-A-Lula [US#7, 1956]
Major Hits: Be-Bop-A-Lula [1956], Lotta' Lovin [1957], Dance To The Bop [1958]

Jerry Lee Lewis' 1957 hit, 'Whole Lotta Shakin' Going On', which sold over six million copies in the first year after its release, was recorded in just one take.

Having being billed as support to an act he felt was far inferior, Jerry Lee once climaxed his act by pouring lighter fuel over the piano and setting fire to it. He then challenged "any son of a bitch" to follow that.

DON'T KNOCK THE ROCK

Rock'n'roll came in for some hysterical criticism right from the start.

"I don't think youth wants this sort of thing. It is the result of the let-down that follows every war" said a New York church minister in 1956, talking about the music of Elvis Presley.

Crooner Frank Sinatra was notoriously vitriolic about rock music in *Western World* magazine in 1957, calling it "The most brutal, ugly, desperate, vicious form of expression it has been my displeasure to hear," continuing "It smells phoney and false. It is sung, played and written for the most part by cretinous goons." And he didn't stop there – "It manages to be the martial music of every sideburned delinquent on the face of the earth. This rancid smelling aphrodisiac I deplore."

At a government hearing in the mid-Fifties, songwriter Billy Rose (responsible for the lyrics "Barney Google, with the goo-goo-googly eyes") thought most of the new songs were "Junk . . . in many cases they are obscene junk pretty much on a level with dirty comic magazines," describing rock'n'rollers as "A set of untalented twisters and twitchers whose appeal is largely to the zootsuiter and the juvenile delinquent."

At the same hearing U.S. Congressman Emanuel Celler was more condescending: "Rock and roll has its place, there's no question about it. It's given great impetus to talent, particularly among the colored people. It's a natural expression of their emotions and gyrations."

And in 1958 St. Louis radio station KWK had all rock'n'roll banned from its play list. DJs gave every rock'n'roll record in the station library a last spin before smashing it to pieces. The station manager said it was "A simple weeding out of undesirable music."

THE RECORD BUSINESS

Since the beginning, rock'n'roll has always been driven by the record business. The biggest stars – though not *always* the most important – have been measured by hit records, with the charts the ultimate slide rule of success.

The Recording Industry Association of American began certifying recordings as *Gold* on March 14th, 1958 to recognize records that sold over 500,000 copies. In 1976, because of booming record sales, the RIAA created a new Platinum award, for singles that sell in excess of 2 million copies and an album that sells 1 million units.

═══ THE BEST SELLING ═══ RECORDS OF ALL TIME

Not every mega-selling single or album has been a rock record of course, as the charts overleaf illustrate. In fact the first record to sell over a million copies was back in 1902, a 78rpm disc of opera star Enrico Caruso singing 'Vesti la Giubba'. But what the charts do demonstrate is the general dominance of rock and rock-related material through the past half century of popular music.

THE TOP TEN SINGLES

1	Candle In The Wind (Diana Tribute)	Elton John	37m
2	White Christmas	Bing Crosby	30m
3	Rock Around The Clock	Bill Haley and His Comets	17m
4	I Want To Hold Your Hand	The Beatles	12m
5	Hey Jude	The Beatles	10m
6	It's Now Or Never	Elvis Presley	10m
7	I Will Always Love You	Whitney Houston	10m
8	Hound Dog	Elvis Presley	9m
9	Diana	Paul Anka	9m
10	(Every Thing I Do) I Do It For You	Bryan Adams	8m

(all sales figures as of November 2004)

THE TOP TEN ALBUMS

(sales in millions)

US

1	Their Greatest Hits (Vol. 1)	The Eagles	28 m
2	Thriller	Michael Jackson	26 m
3	The Wall	Pink Floyd	23 m
4	Led Zeppelin IV	Led Zeppelin	22 m
5	Greatest Hits Vol I & II	Billy Joel	21 m
6	The Beatles	The Beatles	19 m
7	Back In Black	AC/DC	19 m
8	Rumours	Fleetwood Mac	19 m
9	Boston	Boston	17 m
10	The Beatles 1967 - 1970	The Beatles	16 m

UK

1.	Sgt Pepper's Lonely Hearts Club Band	The Beatles	4.5 m
2	(What's The Story) Morning Glory	Oasis	4.2m
3	Brothers In Arms	Dire Straits	3.9 m
4	Bad	Michael Jackson	3.9 m
5	The Immaculate Collection	Madonna	3.6 m
6	Abba Gold Greatest Hits	Abba	3.6 m
7	Stars	Simply Red	3.6 m
8	Thriller	Michael Jackson	3.3 m
9.	Greatest Hits (Volume One)	Queen	3.3 m
10.	Jagged Little Pill	Alanis Morissette	3.0 m

GLOBAL

1	Thriller	Michael Jackson	54m
2	Black In Black	AC/DC	42m
3	Their Greatest Hits	The Eagles	41m
4	Saturday Night Fever	Soundtrack	40m
5	The Bodyguard	Soundtrack	37m
6	Bat Out Of Hell	Meat Loaf	37m
7	Dark Side Of The Moon	Pink Floyd	35m
8	Come On Over	Shania Twain	35m
9	Sgt. Pepper's Lonely Hearts Club Band	The Beatles	32m
10	Dirty Dancing	Soundtrack	32m

═ THE AGE OF THE SINGLE ═

Rock music was initially dominated by the 7-inch vinyl 45rpm single, which took over from the more cumbersome (and breakable!) 10-inch shellac 78s in the mid-Fifties, just as rock'n'roll was shaking things up for the first time.

Sales of 45s exploded in the latter half of the Fifties, as rock took off, and got another boost when the Beatles and such triggered a second rock revolution in the Sixties. Producer Phil Spector referred to his epic singles as 'two-minute symphonies', and through to the end of the 20th Century the single provided a format that perfectly embodied much of what rock'n'roll was all about: instant, to-the-point, accessible, of its time – and at best, utterly memorable.

═══ ONE HIT WONDERS ═══

Every era has its share of One Hit Wonders, stars that shone briefly before disappearing forever from the firmament of fame.

Some were significant in their own right, though only charting once. One of early rock's wild men, Screaming Jay Hawkins was an R&B legend when he died in 2000, but only scraped into the charts once, in 1993, with 'Heart Attack And Vine'. Likewise his namesake Ronnie Hawkins made the US charts just once, with 'Mary Lou' in 1959, but his band The Hawks would evolve into country rock giants The Band in the Sixties.

In most cases the memory of the song has far outlived our recollections of the of the artist.

Some memorable One-Hitters who managed to make it to the Number One spot, never again to grace the hallowed heights of the Top Forty.

1956	Dreamweavers	It's Almost Tomorrow
1958	Kalin Twins	When
1959	Jerry Keller	Here Comes Summer
1960	Ricky Valance	Tell Laura I Love Her
1961	The Marcels	Blue Moon
1961	The Highwaymen	Michael
1962	B. Bumble & The Stingers	Nut Rocker
1966	Overlanders	Michelle
1967	Scott McKenzie	San Francisco (Be Sure To Wear Some Flowers In Your Hair)
1968	Crazy World Of Arthur Brown	Fire
1969	Thunderclap Newman	Something In The Air
1969	Zager & Evans	In The Year 2525
1970	Norman Greenbaum	Spirit In The Sky
1970	Matthew's Southern Comfort	Woodstock

COVER VERSIONS

Sometimes cover versions of records have become more successful than the originals, other times you just wonder why they bothered. The Beatles, for instance, made 'Twist And Shout' all their own, and hardly anyone was aware of the Isley Brothers 1962 original, before or since. On the other hand, 'You've Lost That Lovin' Feeling' by the Righteous Brothers was certainly a stand-alone classic, yet Cilla Black covered it regardless. (Although, to be fair, Cilla's version did get to #2 in the UK chart, while the Brothers made the top spot).

In the Fifties Pat Boone famously took various rock'n'roll songs into the charts for the first time – 'Ain't That A Shame', 'Long Tall Sally' and such – with his admittedly anodyne covers.

More recently, the Fugees completely resurrected and reconstructed Roberta Flack's 'Killing Me Softly' in 1996, as did the Brand New Heavies the following year with the James Taylor ballad from 1971 'You Got A Friend'.

British singer Louise made a highly effective modern R&B version of Stealers Wheel's 1973 hit 'Stuck In the Middle With You' in 2001. Which is more than could be said of Atomic Kitten's 'The Tide Is High' the following year, a UK#1 which was a carbon copy arrangement of Blondie's 1980 hit (itself a cover of a mid-Sixties reggae single by John Holt and The Paragons).

There are the covers you never imagined *were* a cover. Sinead O'Connors magnificent 'Nothing Compares 2 U' from 1990, written by Prince, was originally recorded by The Family. Likewise 'I Heard It Through The Grapevine', forever associated with Marvin Gaye, had already been released by Gladys Knight & the Pips two years earlier, in 1967.

And the Rolling Stones launched their success in the singles charts with a series of cover versions. After their debut with Chuck Berry's 'Come On' (which only made #21 in the UK) in July 1963, followed by the Beatles' 'I Wanna Be Your Man' (#12, November '63, though not actually a cover) they made #3 in February 1964 with Buddy Holly's 'Not Fade Away'. Then followed their first two UK chart-toppers, 'It's All Over Now' originally recorded by the Valentinos, and Willie Dixon's 'Little

Red Rooster' (in July and November 1964 respectively). And their first Top Twenty entry in America was with 'Time Is On My Side', previously an R&B hit for Irma Thomas, in November '64. It was twenty months from the Stones' chart debut before they made it big with an original – 'The Last Time' in March 1965.

"Rock'n'Roll is funny – four jerks and a police escort!!"
Bono

"If you tried to give rock and roll another name,
you might call it Chuck Berry"
John Lennon

"Rock and Roll: Music for the neck downwards"
Keith Richards

"As I define it, rock and roll is dead. The attitude isn't dead,
but the music is no longer vital. It doesn't have the same meaning.
The attitude, though, is still very much alive – and it still informs
other kinds of music"
David Byrne

"My my, hey hey, Rock and roll is here to stay"
Neil Young

"I always felt rock and roll was very, very
wholesome music."
Aretha Franklin

"I don't know anything about music.
In my line you don't have to"
Elvis Presley

DEATH DISCS

A macabre sub-genre of rock'n'roll singles, the songs on 'death discs' were usually about car or motorcycle fatalities, though occasionally referred to real-life deceased stars, and always seemed to involve teenagers! The most celebrated death discs were definitely the Shangri Las' 'Leader Of The Pack', Ray Peterson's 'Tell Laura I Love Her' and Bobby Gentry's marvellous 'Ode To Billie Joe'.

1956 **Bill Hayes – Message From James Dean**
A bizarre cash-in on Dean's demise in a car crash.

1958 **Jody Reynolds – Endless Sleep** US#5
Enticed into the sea by his drowned girlfriend – a weird and wonderful record covered in the UK by Marty Wilde.

1960 **Ray Peterson – Tell Laura I Love Her** US#7
Tommy enters a stock-car race to buy his girl a ring... these are his dying words after a fatal smash.

1960 **Mark Dinning – Teen Angel** US#1
Car stalls on railway crossing, boy pulls girl to safety, girl rushes back to retrieve his high school ring......

1961 **Mike Berry – Tribute To Buddy Holly** UK#26
Another pop obituary, this one banned by the BBC fo being in bad taste.

1963 **Heinz – Just Like Eddie** UK#5
Eddie Cochran died in England in 1960, so at least this tribute record wasn't exactly opportunistic.

1964 **Shangri Las – Leader Of The Pack** US#1
Simply the most famous motor cycle death disc of them all.

1964 **Twinkle – Terry** UK#4
A Brit 'Leader Of The Pack', banned by the Beeb.

1965 **Shangri Las – Give Us Your Blessings** US#29
The tale of Mary and Jimmy who elope in Jimmy's car when
they don't get her parents permission to marry. Of course
it's raining (cue thunder) and they don't see the detour sign
(cue crash)

1967 **Bobbie Gentry – Ode To Billie Joe** US#1
The eerie tale, told in a matter-of-fact way around the
dinner table ("…pass the biscuits please") of Billy Joe's
suicide off the Tallahatchie Bridge.

BANNED!

Since the advent of records and radio, music has come in for
some stern censorship from time to time. Finding it almost
impossible to stop actual discs being recorded, manufactured
and sold, the free proliferation of music via radio was a pefect
opportunity for moralists of various persuasions to impose
bans.

In the early rock'n'roll era, some US DJs were notorious for
their public destruction of the discs they had banned – in one
case just Elvis platters, nothing else. Even in the swinging
Sixties, after John Lennon made his "we're more popular than
Jesus" remark, Beatles records were burned by a number of
American radio stations.

In Britain, most music censorship in the Fifties was via the
BBC as the only broadcasting organisation. Famous bans by
the Beeb back then included Johnnie Ray's 'Such A Night' and

The Best Of The Banned

Year	Artist	Title	Reason Banned
1954	Johnnie Ray	Such A Night	*Sexually explicit*
1956	Nervous Norvus	Transfusion	*Bad taste*
1956	Lonnie Donegan	Diggin' My Potatoes	*Sexually explicit*
1957	Everly Brothers	Wake Up Little Susie	*Sexually explicit*
1958	John Zacherle	Dinner With Drac	*Bad taste*
1959	Bobby Darin	Mack The Knife	*Inciting violence*
1960	Ray Peterson	Tell Laura I Love Her	*Morbid*
1961	Mike Berry	Tribute to Buddy Holly	*Bad taste*
1961	Gene McDaniels	100 Pounds Of Clay	*Blasphemous*
1967	Beatles	A Day In The Life	*Drug references*
1968	Rolling Stones	Street Fighting Man	*Political*
1970	Crosby, Stills, Nash & Young	Ohio	*Political*
1971	Beatles	Yellow Submarine	*Drug references*
1976	Rod Stewart	Tonight's The Night	*Sexually explicit*
1977	Sex Pistols	God Save The Queen	*Political*
1983	Frankie Goes To Hollywood	Relax	*Sexually explicit*
1990	Madonna	Justify My Love	*Sexually explicit*
2001	John Lennon	Imagine	*Insensitive post-9/11*
2001	Dave Clark Five	Bits and Pieces	*Insensitive post-9/11*
2001	Buddy Holly	That'll Be the Day	*Insensitive post-9/11*

Lonnie Donegan's 'Diggin' My Potatoes', both for being sexually explicit.

Even in more enlightened times, sex has been the most sensitive area to attract the scrutiny of those determined to protect the rest of us from corrupting influences. 'Relax' by Frankie Goes To Hollywood ran into problems, as did Madonna's 'Justify My Love' video (with visual references to sado-masochism, homosexuality and cross-dressing) on the MTV network.

Politics has been another area often targetted. Paul McCartney's 'Give Ireland Back To The Irish' raised a lot of hackles, though not as much as 'God Save The Queen' by the Sex Pistols, which despite being banned by the all-powerful BBC prior to the Queen's Silver Jubilee made it to #2 in the UK charts.

After the terrorist attacks on the World Trade Center in New York, Clear Channel, the biggest network of US radio stations published a list of songs considered 'insensitive' for DJs to play in the aftermath of the tragedy. These included such items as John Lennon's 'Imagine', 'Leaving On A Jet Plane' by Peter, Paul and Mary, Jerry Lee Lewis with 'Great Balls Of Fire' and the Drifters' 'On Broadway'!

And good old bad taste has been cited more than once as a reason for regulating what we listen to, from death discs (and near-death in the case of 'Transfusion' by Nervous Norvus) to John Zacherle's full-on 'Dinner With Drac', with its lyrics straight out of a Fifties horror comic: "For dessert there was batwing confetti / And the veins of a mummy named Betty / I first frowned upon it / But with ketchup on it / It tasted very much like spaghetti!"

THE FIRST
ROCK'N ROLL ALBUMS

Rock albums as self-contained bodies of work didn't really come into their own until the mid-Sixties. Up till the era of the Beatles, most rock albums consisted either of 'greatest hits' packages, or conversely collections of tracks that would subsequently appear as singles and EPs as well.

The album charts during the early years of rock'n'roll were dominated by film and stage musicals. Of the top ten best sellers of the decade, no less than seven – *South Pacific, Love Me Or Leave Me, My Fair Lady, The Music Man, Around The World In 80 Days, Gigi* and *Peter Gunn* – were original stage casts or soundtrack recordings.

In fact in a list of 35 Top US Albums of the Fifties (as listed in *Billboard* magazine based on their chart positions and weeks at #1), only five were rock'n'roll collections, and four of those were by Elvis Presley – the other being a Ricky Nelson LP, *Ricky*.

Outside the best sellers, the biggest market for non-classical music on album was in the jazz field, and to a lesser extent folk music and blues. *The* trendy 12-inch long-players to be seen with around the end of the Fifties included albums by Dave Brubeck, the Modern Jazz Quartet, Ella Fitzgerald and Ray Charles.

Of the rock artists who *did* make the album charts in the Fifties, these were the biggest sellers:

Name	Album	Year	Chart peak
Bill Haley	Rock Around The Clock	1956	US #12
	Rock'n'Roll Stage Show	1956	US #18
Fats Domino	Rock And Rollin'	1956	US #17
	This Is Fats Domino!	1957	US #19
Elvis Presley	Elvis Presley	1956	US #1, UK#4
	Elvis	1956	US #1
	Loving You	1957	US #1
	Elvis' Christmas Album	1957	US #1
	Elvis' Golden Records	1958	US #3, UK #3
	King Creole	1958	US #2, UK#4
	For LP Fans Only	1959	US #19
Gene Vincent	Bluejean Bop!	1956	US #16
The Platters	The Platters	1956	US #7
	The Platters Vol Two	1957	US #12
	Remember When?	1959	US #15
Little Richard	Here's Little Richard	1957	US #13
Frankie Lymon	The Teenagers featuring Frankie Lymon	1957	US #19
Ricky Nelson	Ricky	1957	US #1
	Ricky Nelson	1958	US #7
	Ricky Sing Again	1959	US #14
Everly Brothers	The Everly Brothers	1958	US #16
Sam Cooke	Sam Cooke	1958	US #16
Buddy Holly	The Buddy Holly Story	1959	US #11, UK#2

THE ALBUM TAKES OFF

In the first half of the Sixties, two names that would change the face of rock music also signalled a move towards albums as part of that change – The Beatles and Bob Dylan.

When it was released in the UK in March 1963, the Beatles' debut LP followed the traditional pattern in that it included both sides of their first two singles, and was titled after their first big UK hit, *Please Please Me*.

But from then on in, the Fab Four from Liverpool – not for the only time – turned conventional practice on its head. Their second album *With The Beatles* didn't include one single track that was released as a UK single, and this was their policy – apart from an "oldies" compilation – almost to the end of their recording career.

A new Beatles album was an event in the mid-Sixties, on a par with their much-anticipated single releases – with both topping their respective charts with phenomenal regularity.

Parallel to the emergence of the Beatles, the other unique voice of Sixties rock appeared, with the emphasis of his work very much in the context of the long-player – Bob Dylan. From being a cult folk artist with his eponymous first album in 1962, Dylan's output from the start was LP-driven. His singles – the biggest being 'Like A Rolling Stone' in 1965, a US #2 as was 'Rainy Day Women #12 & 35' the following year – were always secondary to his ground-breaking LPs. Albums like *Bringing It All Back Home*, *Highway 61 Revisited* and *Blonde On Blonde* came to define the era – and rock music – as much as anything by The Beatles, The Rolling Stones and the rest.

By the end of the Sixties, even though most of its biggest names (with the exception of Dylan) were the major sellers in the singles charts through the decade, the album had become the defining format, the driving force in rock'n'roll.

THE CONCEPT ALBUM

The idea of an album featuring songs with a common theme was nothing new – Frank Sinatra did it several times in the Fifties with titles like *Songs For Swinging Lovers*, *Only For The Lonely* and *In The Wee Wee Hours* – but until the album started to have prominence in the late Sixties, it was unknown in rock'n'roll.

The Beatles' *Sgt. Pepper's Lonely Hearts Club Band* has always been regarded as the first rock concept album. Although the songs didn't have a common subject, the introduction and reprise of the 'Pepper' theme, the smooth segue between tracks and the dubbed-on 'audience ' applause gave it an overall feel of being one piece of work. Plus the packaging of course, with John, Paul, George and Ringo in full Pepper regalia on the cover and inside the gatefold sleeve (another rock first), plus a pull-out of of Pepper cut-outs and all the lyrics on the back sleeve (another innovation). The rock album had not only become an event, but a tangible object you could look at, hold and read, as well as listen to.

In that same year of 1967, the Who released what was in many ways more of a genuine concept album, *The Who Sell Out*, The theme was a pirate radio station that plays nothing but Who songs, complete with radio jingles & commercials (some genuine, some created by the band) sprinkled inbetween the tunes.

And the Who were also responsible for what many consider the most successful of all 'concept' projects, although it was touted as a 'rock opera', the story of the deaf, dumb and blind kid *Tommy* that went on to be a high profile movie.

With the onset of 'progressive rock' in the Seventies, however, concept albums began to get something of a bad name when bands like Yes, Emerson Lake and Palmer, and Pink Floyd worked the idea to death, and came up with some of the most pretentious 'concepts' in the bargain.

MOST PRETENTIOUS CONCEPT ALBUMS... EVER

Deep Purple **Concerto For Group And Orchestra**
1973
Live at the Royal Albert Hall with Royal Philharmonic Orchestra

Emerson, Lake & Palmer **Pictures At An Exhibition**
1972
Based on classical composition by Mussorgsky

Rick Wakeman **Journey To The Centre Of The Earth**
1974
Based on Jules Verne novel, with London Symphony Orchestra

Yes **Tales From Topographic Oceans**
1974
Lyrics based on Shastric scriptures

Camel **The Snow Goose**
1975
Inspired by Paul Gallico's children's novel

TEN ALL-TIME ALBUM CLASSICS

ELVIS PRESLEY – ELVIS PRESLEY 1956
Original Label: RCA Victor [US]
Producer: Sam Phillips / Steve Sholes
US Album Chart: #1 **UK Album Chart:** #4 (1959 reissue)
Elvis' debut album, and what a debut! As well as sensational
versions of Carl Perkins' 'Blue Suede Shoes', Little Richard's
'Tutti Frutti' and Ray Charles' 'I Got A Woman', there are
five tracks recorded at Sun Records before the "Hillbilly
Cat" signed with RCA.

JAMES BROWN – LIVE AT THE APOLLO 1963
Original Label: King [US]
Producer: Tom Nola
US Album Chart: #2
Recorded live at Harlem's famed Apollo Theater, this is 40
minutes of "Mr Dynamite" at his early Sixties prime. The
most sensational live show in soul – featuring classics like
'I'll Go Crazy' and 'Please Please Please' – captured as it
happened.

BOB DYLAN – BRINGING IT ALL BACK HOME 1965
Original Label: Columbia [US]
Producer: Tom Wilson
US Album Chart: #6 **UK Album Chart:** #1
With 'Subterranean Homesick Blues', 'She Belongs To Me',
'Maggie's Farm', 'Mr Tambourine Man' and 'It's All Over Now
Baby Blue' among them, this could be a "best of" album,
there are so many masterpieces on it.

OTIS REDDING – OTIS BLUE 1965
Original Label: Volt [US]
Producer: Jim Stewart
UK Album Chart: #6
The epitome of Sixties soul, including Sam Cooke's 'Shake',
the Stones' 'Satisfaction' and Redding originals 'Respect' and
the marvellous 'I've Been Loving You Too Long'.

BEACH BOYS – PET SOUNDS 1966
Original Label: Capitol
Producer: Brian Wilson
US Album Chart: #10   **UK Album Chart:** #2
Inspired by the Beatles' *Revolver*, Brian Wilson crafted an
album – with tracks including 'Wouldn't It Be Nice' and the
unforgettable 'God Only Knows' – that heralded a break-
through in recording techniques as sensational as anything
happening in England at the time.

BEATLES – SGT PEPPER'S LONELY HEARTS CLUB BAND
1967
Original Label: Parlophone [UK]
Producer: George Martin
US Album Chart: #1 **UK Album Chart:** #1
Forget the "concept" trimmings, this still works simply as a
collection of great tracks, with 'A Little Help From My
Friends', 'Lucy In The Sky With Diamonds', 'Getting Better'
and 'A Day In The Life' as fresh as when they were recorded
nearly forty years ago.

CAROLE KING – TAPESTRY 1971
Original Label: Ode [US]
Producer: Lou Adler
US Album Chart: #1 **UK Album Chart:** #4
A stunning collection from the one-time Brill Building singer

and songwriter, a dozen self-penned numbers – including a new version of the early Sixties 'Will You Love Me Tomorrow' – with James Taylor and a line-up of star session players.

STEVIE WONDER – TALKING BOOK 1972
Original Label: Tamla [US]
Producer: Stevie Wonder
US Album Chart: #3 **UK Album Chart:** #16
As well as the mainstream hit 'You Are The Sunshine Of My Life', this is Stevie stretching himself magnificently, the stand-out tracks being the super-soul of 'Superstition' and the hypnotic 'I Believe (When I Fall In Love It Will Be Forever)'.

BLONDIE – PARALLEL LINES 1978
Original Label: Chrysalis
Producer: Mike Chapman
US Album Chart: #6 **UK Album Chart:** #1
With songs like 'Hanging On The Telephone', 'Sunday Girl' and 'Heart Of Glass', Debbie Harry and the boys prove why they were the best of the groups to come out of the post-punk New York New Wave.

PAUL SIMON – GRACELAND 1986
Original Label: Warner Brothers
Producer: Paul Simon
US Album Chart: #3 **UK Album Chart:** #1
Paul Simon's celebrated liasion with members of the South African musical scene. It's a stunning set with songs like 'The Boy In The Bubble', 'Diamonds On The Soles Of Her Shoes' and the emotive title track, and a rock-based building block for an awareness of "world music".

ARCHITECTS OF ROCK THE PIONEER PRODUCERS

Willie Dixon (b. 1915, d.1992) Key producer at Chess records in Chicago, he worked with all the great blues and R&B artists on the label including Muddy Waters, Howlin Wolf, Sonny Boy Williamson, Bo Diddley and many others.

Milt Gabler (b.1911, d.2001) Famously produced 'Rock Around The Clock' and other hits for Bill Haley, helping define one of the sounds that created rock'n'roll music.

George Goldner (b.1918, d.1970) A classic rock'n'roll entrepreneur, Goldner cut wonderful records in pursuit of the next buck. After hitting R&B gold dust with 'Gee' by The Crows in 1954, he put New York doo-wop firmly on the map with hits by The Chantels, The Cleftones, Little Anthony and the Imperials, The Flamingos and Frankie Lymon and the Teenagers. And although his motives were as monetary as they were musical, he did, as one writer put it, "more for integration than the Supreme Court".

Berry Gordy (b.1929) Creator of the Motown sound, the Detroit label's founder produced or co-produced hits for Smokey Robinson & The Miracles, Mary Wells, The Supremes, the Four Tops, Stevie Wonder and many more.

John Hammond (b.1910, d.1987) His career spanned jazz and rock'n'roll, producing Bessie Smith, Count Basie, Benny Goodman, Bille Holliday (who he discovered), Bob Dylan (who he also discovered), Aretha Franklin and Bruce Springsteen among many, mostly for the Columbia label.

George Martin (b.1926) In his studio work with The Beatles, Martin really was the "fifth" member of the group. The innovations they wrought record by record, from 1963 to 1968, directly influenced the sound of recorded rock everywhere.

Les Paul (b. 1915) His influence on popular music has been huge. As well as inventing the solid-bodied electric guitar, which Gibson produced bearing his name, his innovations in both playing and recording the instrument, and his parallel development of multiple recording, would revolutionize the sound of rock and pop forever.

Sam Phillips (b.1923, d.2003) Founder of Sun Records in Memphis who, before producing the first records by Elvis Presley, was responsible for what many consider the first-ever rock'n'roll record, Jackie Brenston's 'Rocket '88" in 1951. As creator of the Sun rockabilly sound, he also introduced the world to the likes of Johnny Cash, Carl Perkins, Jerry Lee Lewis and Roy Orbison.

Phil Spector (b.1940) Pioneer of the "wall of sound" that characterized early Sixties rock with studio-created girl groups including The Ronettes and The Crystals. He called these records "little symphonies for the kids", but his epic master-pieces were later in the decade, Ike & Tina Turner's 'River Deep, Mountain High' and 'You've Lost That Loving Feeling' by The Righteous Brothers. He went on to have mixed success with ex-Beatles projects, best of which was John Lennon's *Rock'n'Roll* of 1975.

Jerry Wexler (b 1917) Cornerstone of the Atlantic Records R&B sound of the Fifties with Ruth Brown, Ray Charles, Joe Turner, The Coasters et al. Moved south with the label in Sixties, masterminding hits from Memphis and Muscle Shoals, Alabama with artists like Wilson Pickett and Aretha Franklin. His portfolio went on to include Dusty Springfield, Willie Nelson, Dire Straits and Bob Dylan in a career that spans the history of rock'n'roll.

THE MUSIC

ACID ROCK

The term was first applied to early "psychedelic" bands in the mid-Sixties, most prominently the Thirteenth Floor Elevators from Texas, and Jefferson Airplane and the Grateful Dead in California. In fact the 'Elevators were one of the first to refer to their music as psychedelic, naming their debut album *The Psychedelic Sounds Of The Thirteenth Floor Elevators* in 1966.

Acid bands predominated on the San Francisco hippy scene, "stoned" sounding records and live appearances utilizing feedback, fuzz boxes and other effects to distort the sound, imitating the way hallucinogenics like LSD and marijuana altered sensual experience. The Grateful Dead often went on stage totally stoned, taking ages just to tune up, though usually in front of audiences who were equally "out of it".

As 1967's Summer of Love exploded in a haze of flower power, the Beatles, Beach Boys and other formerly "straight" pop bands spread the psychedelic message worldwide, with an "all you need is love" optimism that was as much about visual style as musical substance.

BRILL BUILDING

Successors to the old "Tin Pan Alley" songwriting tradition of New York City, the Brill Building at 1619 Broadway, near the corner with 49th Street, was the home of a "hit factory" of songwriters, publishers and record producers through the late Fifties and early Sixties.

Bridging the gap which had become apparent between traditional songwriting and rock'n'roll music, three young teams of composers emerged who would help change the face of pop – Gerry Goffin and Carole King, Barry Mann and Cynthia Weill, and Neil Sedaka and Howard Greenfield.

TWELVE OF THE BRILL BUILDING'S BIGGEST

Year / Composers / Title / Artist / Charts

1959 Sedaka / Greenfield **Oh Carol!** Neil Sedaka US#9, UK#3

1960 Leiber / Stoller **Save The Last Dance For Me** Drifters US#1, UK#2

1960 Goffin / King **Will You Love Me Tomorrow** Shirelles US#1, UK#4

1961 Leiber / Stoller **Stand By Me** Ben E King US#4, UK#1

1961 Sedaka / Greenfield **Breaking Up Is Hard To Do** N.Sedaka US#1, UK#7

1962 Goffin / King **Up On The Roof** Drifters US#5

1962 Bacharach / David **Baby Its You** Shirelles US#8

1962 Goffin / King **The Locomotion** Little Eva US#1, UK#2

1963 Greenwich / Barry **Da Doo Ron Ron** Crystals US#3, UK#5

1963 Greenwich / Barry **Be My Baby** Ronettes US#2, UK#4

1964 Bacharach / David **Walk On By** Dionne Warwick US#6, UK#9

1964 Spector/Mann /Weill **You've Lost That Loving Feeling** Righteous Bros. US#1, UK#1

Other teams who soon joined them in the Brill Building included Jeff Barry and Ellie Greenwich, Doc Pomus and Morty Schuman, Burt Bacharach and Hal David, and the already high-profile. Jerry Leiber and Mike Stoller. And via Leiber and Stoller, the young Phil Spector was honing his writing and producing craft in and around the Brill.

Through the late Fifties and early Sixties the Brill Building was responsible for more hits than any other single location in rock history.

BRITISH BEAT

Although initially identified with Liverpool in the wake of The Beatles' success, and that of other "Merseybeat" groups such as Gerry & The Pacmakers and The Searchers through 1963, the beat group phenomenon soon manifest itself nationwide with outfits emerging from every corner of the country, from Glasgow's Lulu & The Luvvers to Manchester's Hollies, Newcastle's Animals and Tottenham's Dave Clark Five. Most importantly, it changed the focus of a music industry hitherto dominated by formulaic pop, created in the main by songwriters and publishers in London's Tin Pan Alley.

Like the Liverpool bands (including the Beatles before Lennon and McCartney's songwriting talents put them in a league of their own), most of the beat groups specialized in pared-down guitar-driven covers of American R&B pop. By the end of 1964, London's Rolling Stones (with more emphasis on "pure" rhythm and blues) had become the only serious rivals to the Beatles, who by that time were spearheading the British Beat "invasion" of the United States which would change the course of pop music forever.

Profile: THE BEATLES

JOHN LENNON

Born: John Winston Lennon, 9 October 1940, Liverpool UK

Died: 8 December 1980, New York City, NY

PAUL MCCARTNEY

Born: James Paul McCartney, 18 June 1942, Liverpool UK

GEORGE HARRISON

Born: George Harrison, 25 February 1943, Liverpool UK

Died: 29 November 2001, Los Angeles, California

RINGO STARR:

Born: Richard Starkey, 7 July 1940, Liverpool UK

Chart Debut: Love Me Do [UK#17, 1962]

Major Hits: Please Please Me, From Me To You, She Loves You, I Want To Hold Your Hand[1963], Can't Buy Me Love, Do You Want To Know A Secret ,A Hard Day's Night, I Feel Fine, [1964], Eight Days A Week, Ticket To Ride, Help!, Yesterday, Day Tripper/ We Can Work It Out [1965], Paperback Writer, Yellow Submarine/Eleanor Rugby [1966], Penny Lane/ Strawberry Fields Forever, All You Need Is Love, Hello Goodbye, Magical Mystery Tour [1967], Lady Madonna, Hey Jude [1968], Get Back, Ballad Of John And Yoko, Something/ Come Together [1969], Let It Be, The Long And Winding Road [1970] **Major Albums:** With The Beatles [1963], Rubber Soul [1965], Revolver [1966], Sgt Pepper's Lonely Hearts Club Band [1967].

Facts'n'Figures: When, on Sunday 10 February 1964, the Beatles made their first appearance on the Ed Sullivan show on US television, there were over 73 million viewers, with over 45 percent of all sets in America tuned in. Allegedly that night the crime rate among American teenagers plumetted to almost zero.

ROCKCITY: LIVERPOOL

Location: North west England, on the Irish Sea at the mouth of the River Mersey. Previously in the county of Lancashire, now the hub of the metropolitan area of Merseyside. Thirty miles west of its traditional rival Manchester.

Musical Milestones: Birthplace of the Beatles, and centre of the Mersey "sound" that kick-started British Beat in the early Sixties. Before that, in the late Fifties produced one of the UK's best pre-beat rockers Billy Fury. Liverpool also saw a local renaissance in the early Eighties with bands like Echo And The Bunnymen, Teardrop Explodes, Orchestral Manouvres In The Dark and the hugely successful Frankie Goes To Hollywood. Most recently girl group Atomic Kitten have graced the charts with a series of pop hits.

Also Famous For: Football teams (Liverpool and Everton), poets (Henri, McGough, Patten), playwrites (Willie Russell, Alan Bleasedale), comedians (visit any pub) and the late John Peel.

Biggest Names: Billy Fury, Beatles, Searchers, Gerry & The Pacemakers, Billy J Kramer, Cilla Black, Scaffold, Echo And The Bunnymen, Teardrop Explodes, Orchestral Manouvres In The Dark, Dead Or Alive, Frankie Goes To Hollywood, Elvis Costello, The La's, Boo Radleys, Melanie C, Atomic Kitten.

Historic Places:
The Cavern, 10 Mathew Street. The re-opened Cavern is
   actually a few doors up from the original site.
Ye Cracke, Rice Street. Old "art student" pub, early Lennon
   hang-out, still open.
Eric's, Mathew Street. The main post-punk "renaissance"
   venue – defunct.
Hope Hall basement, Hope Street. Sixties R&B and poetry

venue – now the Everyman Theatre, still with a basement
  club / restaurant.
The Iron Door, Temple Street. Sixties beat scene venue –
  defunct.
Jacaranda coffee bar, Slater Street. An early Beatle hang-out
  and venue – reopened.
Penny Lane – just catch the 86 bus.
Strawberry Fields, Beaconsfield Road, Woolton. A childrens'
  home until it closed in June 2005.

BRIT POP

Something of a catch-all term covering a broad movement of
guitar-led pop-oriented British rock bands in the mid-Nineties
Prime instigators were Blur, who drew on classic UK pop by
the likes of The Kinks. Their 1994 album *Parklife* included a
string of single hits including one of their biggest, 'Girls And
Boys'.

1994 also saw the emergence of Manchester rockers Oasis,
similarly inspired by Sixties guitar pop, most specifically The
Beatles. Much tougher in their sound (and image) than Blur,
both groups were locked into a much-hyped feud, billed by the
media as the "battle of the bands" in mid-1995 when both
bands released a single on the same day. In the event Blur won
the day with 'Country House' hitting #1, while Oasis' 'Roll
With It' tailed them at #2. Oasis , however, had four of their
next six singles topping the chart, the other two making
second place, and two #1 albums in 1994 and 1995.

The enigmatic Jarvis Cocker fronted the third of Brit Pop's big
three, Pulp. His oblique and witty observations on suburban
life were best captured on their million-selling album *Different
Class* and the spin-off singles 'Common People' and 'Mis-
Shapes / Sorted For E's And Whizz', both UK #2s.

With other guitar bands like Supergrass, Elastica, Suede ("London Suede" in the US), The Verve and Boo Radleys all enjoying chart status in the mid-Nineties, the Britpop phenomenon, though largely limited to within UK shores, nevertheless impacted on US rock'n'roll groups like The Strokes and Interpol who rejuvinated the New York scene in the early 2000s.

BEST OF THE BRITS

1994 Suede	Coming Up	UK#1 [album]
1994 Blur	Parklife	UK#1 [album]
1994 Blur	Girls And Boys	UK#5
1994 Oasis	Definitely Maybe	UK#1 [album]
1995 Blur	Country House	UK#1
1995 Boo Radleys	Wake Up!	UK#1 [album]
1995 Oasis	Roll With It	UK#2
1995	(What's The Story) Morning Glory?	UK#1 [album]
1995 Oasis	Wonderwall	UK#2
1995 Pulp	Common People	UK#2
1995 Pulp	Different Class	UK#1 [album]
1995 Supergrass	I Should Coco	UK#1 [album]
1995 Elastica	Elastica	UK#1 [album]
1996 Oasis	Don't Look Back In Anger	UK#1
1995 Elastica	Elastica	UK#1 [album]
1997 The Verve	The Drugs Don't Work	UK#1
1997 The Verve	Urban Hymns	UK#1 [album]

"I'm the Connie Francis of rock 'n' roll"
Elton John

"We're more popular than Jesus now; I don't know which will go first, rock 'n' roll or Christianity"
John Lennon

COUNTRY ROCK

Right from the earliest days, rock'n'roll was closely linked to country music, or hillbilly music as it was originally dubbed. Indeed, the very first recordings by Elvis, Carl Perkins and other pioneering rockers at Sun Records and elsewhere were labelled "rockabilly", illustrating that connection. And some of Elvis' greatest sides when he moved to RCA were made in their Nashville studios with country guitar maestro Chet Atkins at the production desk.

Through the Fifties rock and country went their separate paths, though stars like the Everly Brothers and Buddy Holly managed to inject the former with strong hints of the latter. But by the middle Sixties, country music *per se* had become marginalized from mainstream rock, caricatured as whining, sentimental music sung by rednecks in big hats and bouffant-haired women in spangly cowgirl outfits.

Former folk-rock group The Byrds – with the legendary Gram Parsons in their line-up – released the very first country rock album in 1968, *Sweetheart Of The Rodeo*.

In 1969 Bob Dylan surprised many by recording an album with guest appearances by country legend Johnny Cash, *Nashville Skyline*. It shouldn't have come as that much of a culture shock, given that Cash had his roots in rock'n'roll as a leading name on Sun Records, and Dylan's background was in American folk music.

Dylan's backing group The Band went on to spearhead country rock, which developed through the Seventies in albums by the likes of Emmylou Harris, Steve Earle, Kris Kristofferson and the "outlaw" country artists led by Willie Nelson and Waylon Jennings.

The Cohen Brothers' 2000 movie *O Brother, Where Art Thou?* triggered a 21st century boom in rock-tinged bluegrass music with hit albums by such artists as Gillian Welch and Alison Krauss.

COUNTRY ROCK CLASSICS

1968	Sweetheart Of The Rodeo	The Byrds
1969	Nashville Skyline	Bob Dylan
1969	The Band	The Band
1976	The Outlaws	Waylon Jennings, Willie Nelson, Jessi Colter, Tompall Glaser
1976	Elite Hotel	Emmylou Harris

═══════ DANCE CRAZES ═══════

Dance crazes – and some crazy dances – had been around before the beginning of rock'n'roll, with jitterbug and jiving in the dance halls of the Forties.

During the early 1950s, the Creep was banned from many ballrooms on account of the "lewd" nature of the close-contact shuffling steps involved.

Johnny Otis' 'Willie And The Hand Jive', dedicated to the Fifties dance you could do sitting down, was subsequently covered by Cliff Richard and (in the Seventies) Eric Clapton.

The most celebrated new dance in the early Sixties was the Twist. Originated on a record by Hank Ballard that made the charts worldwide in a cover by Chubby Checker, it was further popularized by the crowds at New York's trendy Peppermint Lounge.

Chubby Checker got his big break as a replacement for Hank Ballard when the original Twist man didn't show up for a TV show.

Other crazes that came in the wake of the Twist, but nowhere as near popular, included the Mashed Potato, the Locomotion, the Hucklebuck and the Wah Watusi – not to forget the Frug, the Pony, the Funky Chicken and the Turkey Trot!

Husband-and-wife songwriters Gerry Goffin and Carole King recruited their baby sitter Eva Boyd (hereafter known as Little Eva) for 'The Locomotion' that became a much-remembered smash hit.

The first really big dance craze since the Twist was the 8 million-selling record The Hustle by Van McCoy that launched the fashion for disco dancing in 1975.

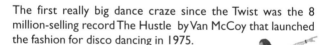

LET'S DANCE!

Willie and the Hand Jive	Johnny Otis	1958
The Stroll	Diamonds	1958
The Twist	Hank Ballard	1960
Wah Watusi	Orlons	1960
Hully Gully Baby	Dovells	1960
Mashed Potato Time	Dee Dee Sharp	1962
Limbo Rock	Chubby Checker	1962
The Locomotion	Little Eva	1962
Walkin' The Dog	Rufus Thomas	1963
The Hustle	Van McCoy	1975

FLOWER POWER

Blossoming in 1967's "summer of love", flower power wasn't just about music but concerned every facet of the drug-influenced "psychedelic" scene. Fashion, graphic design, literature, political attitudes and in many cases the entire lifestyle of the "beautiful people" were changed as a result.

In April, 1967, the Greyhound bus company began offering a guided tour of what they called "Hippyland" – the Haight Ashbury district of San Francisco, considered the epicentre of the counter-culture.

Musically, as well as the hard-core acid bands who instigated much of the change in the first place, it permeated into mainstream rock with everyone from the Beatles and Beach Boys to the Who and the Rolling Stones donning floral kaftans, burning incense and singing of peace'n'love.

The spaced-out performances of many psychedelic bands (see Acid Rock, above) provided a template for the musical excesses of heavy rock prototypes Cream, as well as a platform for the brilliant – though ultimately equally self-indulgent – guitar innovations of Jimi Hendrix.

As well as genuine anthems like the Beatles' 'All You Need Is Love', flower power pop produced vacuous hits like Scott McKenzie's 'San Francisco (Be Sure To Wear Flowers In Your Hair)' in mid-1967, and the UK's ludicrous Flowerpot Men with 'Let's Go To San Francisco' that same crazy summer.

ROCKCITY: SAN FRANCISCO

Location: On the west coast of the United States, overlooking the San Francisco Bay and the Pacific Ocean in northern California.

Musical Milestones: The West Coast psychedelic music revolution was launched in December 1965 when promoter Bill Graham put on a concert of new groups including The Grateful Dead and Great Society, at what would be the Fillmore Auditorium. Through 1966 the scene exploded, centred on the bohemian district of Haight-Ashbury. The Beatles played their final gig at the city's Candlestick Park on 29 August 1966, and in 1967 Graham opened the bigger Fillmore West venue featuring the cream of the new "underground" bands. And a thriving punk scene developed in the Eighties around the hardcore band The Dead Kennedys.

Also Famous For: Beat writers (centred on the City Lights bookshop), cable cars, Golden Gate Bridge, Alcatraz and sudden fog.

Biggest Names: Grateful Dead, Moby Grape, The Great Society, Jefferson Airplane, Creedence Clearwater Revival, Metallica, Dead Kennedys, Primus

Historic Places:

Fillmore Auditorium, 1805 Geary Boulevard/ Fillmore Street. Formerly the Carousel Ballroom before its hippy heyday, it re-opened in 1993

Great American Music Hall, 859 O'Farrell Street. One of the oldest Sixties venues still open.

Avalon Ballroom, Sutter Street/ Van Ness Avnue. With the Fillmore, the most important venue on the mid-Sixties scene, now closed.

Candlestick Park, Candlestick Point, Bayview. Where the Beatles played their last concert, formerly the home of the Giants baseball team. Now known as 3Com and still used for football.

Profile: JIMI HENDRIX

Born: Johnny Allen Hendrix, 27 November 1942, Seattle, Washington

Died: 18 September 1970, London, UK

Chart Debut: Hey Joe [UK#6, 1967]

Major Hits: Purple Haze, The Wind Cries Mary [1967], All Along The Watchtower [1968], Voodoo Chile [1970] **Major Albums:** Are You Experienced? [1967], Axis: Bold As Love, Electric Ladyland [1968]

Facts'n'Figures: Although Hendrix broke through in the UK before his native America, several British record companies had turned down his version of 'Hey Joe', (a cover of a 1966 US hit by The Leaves) before it was finally released by Polydor in early 1967. It made the #6 spot in just ten days.

FOLK ROCK

Folk Rock was largely triggered by Bob Dylan's move from acoustic to electric instrumentation. Dylan's break-through, which famously elicited a shout of "Judas" from a member of the audience during his 1966 British tour, first happened live at the Newport Folk Festival the previous year, when similar howls of derision came from purists in the audience. The Dylan album which defined the genre was 1965's *Bringing It All Back Home*, and his biggest yet, selling over a million copies.

The Lovin' Spoonful, led by John Sebastian, had their roots, like Dylan, in the Greenwich Village folk scene in New York. In 1966 they had three huge hits, 'Daydream' (US#2), 'Did You Ever Have To Make Up Your Mind' (US#2) and 'Summer In The City', which topped the charts.

West Coast guitar band The Byrds made the #1 spot with their rock group version of Dylan's 'Mr Tambourine Man' in June 1965, repeating the feat later in the year with 'Turn Turn Turn', written by folk singer Pete Seeger.

Originating in a New York folk group The Mugwumps, The Mamas And The Papas relocated to California before having their first big hit, appropriately 'Califonia Dreamin', in 1966. followed by their only chart-topper 'Monday, Monday'.

Profile: BOB DYLAN
Born: Robert Allen Zimmerman, 24 May 1941,
    Duluth, Minnesota
Chart Debut: Times They Are A-Changin' [UK#9,
    1965]

Major Hits: Like A Rolling Stone [1965], Rainy Day Women # 12 & 35 [1966], Lay Lady Lay [1969]

Major Albums: Freewheelin' [1964], Bringing It All Back Home, Highway 61 Revisited [1965], Blonde On Blonde [1966], Nashville Skyline [1969], Blood On The Tracks [1975], Oh Mercy [1989], Time out Of Mind [1997]

Facts'n'Figures: There are on record nearly 6,000 cover versions of 350 different Bob Dylan songs, by 2,800 artists! His five most covered songs are 'Blowin' In The Wind' with 375 cover versions, 'Don't Think Twice, It's All Right' with 217, 'I Shall Be Released' [181], 'Mr. Tambourine Man' [176] and 'Like A Rolling Stone' with 172.

GIRL GROUPS

Although all-girl vocal outfits (as opposed to female instrumental bands) have been around since pre-rock lady line-ups like the Andrews Sisters, the golden age of girlie groups was in the early years of the Sixties. Often put together in the studio by Svengali-like producers – including undoubted geniuses such as Phil Spector and Shadow Morton – it was sometimes difficult to tell the Chantels from the Shirelles or the Charmettes from the Marvelettes. But the hundreds of girl group records included many works of wonder, including tasty classics by The Cookies, The Cupcakes, The Honeys and the Jelly Beans – not to mention the incomparable Shangri-Las whose seven-inch sagas included the greatest teen-angst epic of all, the amazing 'Past, Present And Future'.

The legacy of the girl groups lives on. In recent years there have been the Spice Girls, a world-wide phenomenon in the mid-Nineties, All Saints with an all-time classic in 1997's

'Never Ever', and many more rivals of the ubiquitous "boy bands" from Atomic Kitten to Girls Aloud.

TWELVE GIRL GROUP GREATS

Ad Libs	Boy From New York City	1965	US# 8
Angels	My Boyfriend's Back	1963	US# 1
Chiffons	He's So Fine	1963	US# 1
Crystals	Da Doo Ron Ron	1963	US# 3
Dixie Cups	Chapel Of Love	1964	US# 1
Exciters	Tell Him	1962	US# 4
Marvelettes	Please Mr Postman	1961	US# 1
Ronettes	Be My Baby	1963	US# 2
Shangri-Las	Leader Of The Pack	1964	US# 1
Shirelles	Will You Love Me Tomorrow	1960	US# 1
Supremes	Baby Love	1964	US# 1
Toys	A Lover's Concerto	1965	US# 2

The Motown group fronted by Diana Ross weren't the first line-up to call themselves the Supremes. An all-male quartet from Columbus, Ohio used the name on a 1957 single 'Just You And I'. And girl group Ruby & The Romantics, who had a US #1 hit with 'Our Day Will Come' in 1963, started out as The Supremes

The piano on the Shangri-Las' 1965 hit, 'Leader of the Pack' was played by Billy Joel, just 16 years old at the time

When The Shirelles recorded 'Soldier Boy' in one take, as an album filler in 1962, little did they think that a few months later it would be released as a single, climbing to #3 on the R&B chart and #1 on the pop chart, becoming the group's biggest seller.

Although the 1962 chart-topper 'He's A Rebel' was credited by producer Phil Spector to his group The Crystals, they

never sang a note on the record. The song was actually recorded by The Blossoms, featuring Darlene Love – who also sang "ghost" lead with another Spector group, Bob B. Soxx & The Blue Jeans

GLAM ROCK

Glam rock spanned the rock extremes of the early Seventies, ranging from the worst of bubblegum pop to the trendiest in art rock. Dressing up was a knee-jerk reaction (in the tightest of lycra pants of course) to the T-shirt and denim look of increasingly dreary progressive rock, and whether it was the singalong-singles of Sweet and Slade or the knowing camp of Roxy Music and David Bowie, British rock suddenly looked like it was part of the entertainment business again.

In America, initially dubbed "fag rock" it was a harder sell, and although The New York Dolls were seminal in the genesis of punk, the biggest glam band Stateside didn't appear till mid-decade beneath the make-up masks of Kiss.

Bowie did manage to achieve superstar status in America, where Kiss continued to chart into the Eighties, their platform shoes and stage pyrotechnics – though not so much the all-over make-up – creating a template for stadium rockers to come.

Profile: DAVID BOWIE
Born: David Robert Jones, 8 January 1947, London, UK
Chart Debut: Space Oddity [UK#5, 1969]
Major Hits: Jean Genie [1972], Space Oddity, Fame [1975], Ashes To Ashes [1980], Under Pressure

[1981], Let's Dance [1983], Dancing In The Street [1985]

Major Albums: The Rise And Fall Of Ziggy Stardust And The Spiders From Mars, Hunky Dory [1972], Alladin Sane, Pin-Ups [1973], Diamond Dogs [1974], Station To Station [1976], Let's Dance[1983]

Facts'n'Figures: Bowie's first chart record 'Space Oddity' first appeared in the UK chart at #48 in September 1969 for just one week, returning to the list two weeks later for a three month run where it peaked at #5. The album of the same name didn't make the chart until late 1972, when it was first released in '69 as *David Bowie* it failed to make the LP Top 100. The single entered the US chart in February 1973, followed by the album. Then the single re-entered the British chart in October 1975, making the #1 spot. Finally the album hit the UK chart again, in April 1990.

GRUNGE

Grunge could be described as a punk stance applied to a heavy metal dynamic. Seattle band Mudhoney are often referred to as the "godfathers of grunge", but the genre really made its mark with Nirvana, whose early Nineties success was cut short with the suicide of leader Kurt Cobain. Other grunge outfits who emerged in their wake included Pearl Jam, the Foo Fighters, Green Day and Garbage.

Bands from cities around the U.S. Pacific Northwest including Seattle, Washington, Olympia, Washington, and Portland, Oregon, pioneered grunge music and later made it popular with mainstream audiences. Seattle was the most prominent of these centres, due in part to the highly influential Sub Pop label, which released Mudhoney, Nirvana and Soundgarden among a number of crucial bands from the area.

Mark Arm, vocalist with the Seattle band Green River (who later became Mudhoney), is widely thought to be the first person to use the term "grunge" to describe the style, even though he meant it in a negative way. He called the band's style "pure grunge, pure shit".

ROCKCITY: SEATTLE

Location: Pacific North West coast of the United States, in the State of Washington. About a hundred miles south of the Canadian border.

Musical Milestones: Birthplace of Jimi Hendrix, 1942. In the late Forties, the springboard for the careers of both Ray Charles and arranger Quincy Jones. In the rock'n'roll era, the Fleetwoods made it big with two national #1s in 1959, followed by the influential instrumental act The Ventures in the early Sixties. Garage rock oriented around the city in 1963 with North West groups Paul Revere and the Raiders and The Kingsmen competing with rival versions of the legendary 'Louie Louie'. In the Nineties, Seattle was the centre of the "grunge" phenomenon. Since the new millennium, site of the Experience Music Project rock'n'roll museum.

Also Famous For: Aircraft industry (Boeing), coffee (Starbucks), computing (Microsoft), a monorail – and fish.

Biggest Names: Jimi Hendrix, Ventures, Fleetwoods, Queensryche, Soundgarden, Green River, Screaming Trees, Nirvana, Alice In Chains, Mother Love Bone, Mudhoney, Pearl Jam, Foo Fighters

Historic Places:
Crocodile Cafe, 2200 2nd Avenue. A birthplace of grunge
    and still a thriving venue.
Sub Pop, 1932 First Avenue. Headquarters of the grunge
    record label, recently moved.

GUITAR HEROES

The guitar has long been central to the iconography of rock music, since the days of Elvis' early recordings featuring Scotty Moore. Moore, and Chuck Berry, were to inspire a generation of young British players including Eric Clapton, George Harrison and Jimmy Page

The first guitarist to chart regularly as a solo instrumental star was Duane Eddy, whose "twangy" guitar sound (with the heavily-amplified melody played on the bass strings) made over twenty appearances in the UK and US charts between 1958 and 1963. His best sellers included 'Rebel-Rouser', 'Peter Gunn' and – with strings – the emotive 'Because They're Young'. He made the album charts too, his hits there including *Have Twangy Guitar Will Travel*, *A Million Dollars Worth Of Twang* and the marvellously-titled *The Twangs The Thang*.

Guitar-based instrumental groups were also fashionable in the early Sixties. In America the biggest were the Ventures, with hits like the million-selling 'Walk-Don't Run' and 'Perfidia'. And in Britain there were the Shadows, who, as well as being Cliff Richard's regular backing group, clocked up an amazing twenty chart singles in the first half of the decade, including five #1s.

Guitar heroes really came into their own with the British-led rhythm and blues boom, which saw the emergence of virtuoso players like Jimmy Page, Eric Clapton and Jeff Beck. By the end of the Sixties heavier outfits had evolved focusing even more on the guitar front man, most spectacularly Cream featuring Clapton, Led Zeppelin with Page, and of course Jimi Hendrix, whose wizardry on the instrumnent eclipsed anyone before or since.

Profile: ERIC CLAPTON
Born: Eric Clapp, 30 March 1945, Ripley, Surrey UK
Chart Debut: Layla (*as Derek & The Dominos*)
   [UK#7, US#10 1972]
Major Hits: I Shot The Sheriff [1974], Lay Down
   Sally [1976], Tears In Heaven [1992]
Major Albums: Blues Breakers (*John Mayall with Eric
   Clapton*) [1966], 461 Ocean Boulevard [1974],
   Slowhand [1977], Just One Night [1980], August
   [1986], Journeyman [1989], Unplugged [1992],
   From The Cradle [1994]

Facts'n'Figures: Clapton first achieved superstar status in America with Cream. All four albums they released before disbanding in 1969 – *Disraeli Gears*, *Wheels Of Fire*, *Fresh Cream* and *Goodbye* – earned gold records in the States for sales of over half a million.

HEAVY METAL

American band Steppenwolf coined the term in their 1968 hit 'Born To Be Wild', having taken the phrase from the William Burroughs novel *The Naked Lunch*.

A product of the second British blues boom in the late Sixties, heavy metal's godfathers were Cream, Jimi Hendrix and Led Zeppelin. As the music got louder, guitar solos longer, on-stage posing more flamboyant and shows more spectacular, a pattern was established which less skilled blues outfits took on board to make bombastic, no-holds-barred, in-your-face rock.

American metal pioneers of the Seventies included Grand Funk Railroad, Mountain and Blue Oyster Cult, while in Britain the genre flourished courtesy of heavy outfits like Deep Purple, Uriah Heep and Black Sabbath, and later Iron Maiden and Def Leppard.

Metal soon morphed into a perplexing number of sub-categories including pomp rock, thrash metal, grunge and nu-metal, but "mainstream" metal has included AC/DC, Metallica, Motorhead, Van Halen and, more recently, Limp Biskit and Linkin Park.

METAL GUITAR GIANTS

Richie Blackmore	Deep Purple, Rainbow
Tony Iommi	Black Sabbath
Dave Navarro	Red Hot Chili Peppers
Jimmy Page	Led Zeppelin
Glen Tipton	Judas Priest
Eddie Van Halen	Van Halen

Profile: LED ZEPPELIN

JIMMY PAGE
Born: 9 January 1944, Heston, UK
ROBERT PLANT
Born: 20 August 1948, West Bromwich, Birmingham UK
JOHN PAUL JONES
Born: John Baldwin, 3 June 1946, Sidcup, Kent UK
JOHN BONHAM
Born: 31 May 1948, Birmingham UK
Died: 25 September 1980, New York City, NY
Chart Debut: Whole Lotta Love [US#4, 1969]
Major Albums: Led Zeppelin [1969], Led Zeppelin II [1969], Led Zeppelin III [1970], (Led Zeppelin IV) untitled [1971], Houses Of The Holy [1973], Physical Graffiti [1975], Presence, The Song Remains The Same (soundtrack) [1976], In Through The Out Door [1979]

Facts'n'Figures: Led Zeppelin were truly an album band, so much so they never released a single in their native UK until 1997, when 'Whole Lotta Love' (which had sold over half a million in America first time round) from 1969's *Led Zeppelin II* hit the charts. But their long-playing sales were phenomenal, with their first six albums going gold in the United States, followed by platinum honours for the next four.

NEW WAVE

Seventies new wave music could be said to be the grown-up successor to punk, with all the energy of the two-chord nihilistic spikey-heads chanelled into crafted pop with a classic rock'n'roll finesse.

In New York City – the true birthplace of punk – classic new wave included the artful Talking Heads, the quirkiness of the B-52s and the perfect pop of Blondie.

In Britain, the new wave was spearheaded by The Jam (always nearer to a Sixties pop dynamic than their punk rivals), Ian Dury with jazz-infected poetry rock gone a little mad, and the increasingly eclectic Elvis Costello.

PUNK

In the mid-Seventies, punk was a reaction to the indulgences of rock "dinosaurs" like Led Zeppelin and The Rolling Stones, and the superficial narcissism of glam.

Despite assertions to the contrary, New York, not London, was the real birthplace of punk. A year or more before The Sex Pistols, The Clash and such were causing mayhem in

London clubs like The Roxy in 1976, The New York Dolls, Richard Hell, The Ramones and scores more were ripping apart the fabric of rock in Manhattan venues such as CBGB and Max's Kansas City. And Sixties NY band the Velvet Underground were a named inspiration for the punk movement.

A New York fanzine called *Punk* was launched in January 1976, a good eight months before the term was widely used by the UK music press. Issue #4 in the July featured a *Playboy*-style centrefold of Debbie Harry as "*Punk* Playmate of the Month", with a headline that ran "Blondie is the sexiest chick on the New York underground rock scene".

British punk exploded onto the front pages of the tabloid press when The Sex Pistols uttered four-letter expletives in a prime-time TV interview conducted by Bill Grundy. The 'Pistols thrived on their notoriety, as a result being sacked from two labels (EMI and A&M) in a matter of weeks. Then in June 1977 their single 'God Save The Queen', coinciding with the Queen's Silver Jubilee, made #2 in the UK charts despite being banned by the BBC.

The 'Pistols first record contract was with EMI, signed in October 1976, and the band collecting an advance of £40,000. The company dropped them in January 1977. On March 10 1977 they signed with A&M for a £75,000 advance, only to be dropped on March 16 without releasing a record. Then in May '77 they signed to Virgin for an advance of £15,000.

ROCKCITY: NEW YORK

Location: On the North Eastern seaboard of the United States, centred on the island of Manhattan at the mouth of the Hudson river.

Musical Milestones: In the Fifties the base of pioneering rock'n'roll DJ Alan Freed, a centre for doo-wop and at the end of the decade Brill Building pop. Hub of the folk rock boom in the Sixties, similarly with punk in the Seventies – not to mention disco-glam exemplified in trendy Studio 54. Eighties new wave music was based in NYC, as was much avant garde and alternative rock in the Nineties. The city saw a revival in pop rock in the early 2000s, with bands like The Strokes and Interpol.

Also Famous For: Beat writers, abstract painting, skyscrapers, Woody Allen, yellow cabs and breakfast.

Biggest Names: Drifters, Dione & The Belmonts, Carole King, Bob Dylan, Lovin' Spoonful, Simon and Garfunkel, Velvet Underground, Bruce Springsteen, New York Dolls, Ramones, Blondie, Talking Heads, Lou Reed, Sonic Youth, John Spencer, Lenny Kravitz, Strokes, Yeah Yeah Yeahs

Historic Places:

CBGB, 315 Bowery. Punk stronghold since 1975, lease expired 2005

Apollo Theater, 253 West 125th Street. Legendary Harlem venue, the celebrated Wednesday night talent contests still popular

Max's Kanasa City, 240 West 52nd Street. Early punk venue on Park venue, now relocated.

Paramount Theater, 385 Flatbush Avenue, Brooklyn. Cinema venue of first Alan Freed rock'n'roll concert in 1955. Closed 1962, now a gymnasium for Long Island University

Brill Building, 1619 Broadway at 49th Street. Still standing, though no longer a centre of music publishing.

Shea Stadium, 123-01 Roosevelt Avenue, Flushing, Queens. Venue of the Beatles' most famous US appearance, home of the New York Mets baseball team.

═SIXTIES RHYTHM & BLUES═

The R&B boom of the Sixties was based on British beat groups like The Animals and Rolling Stones whose repertoire leaned heavily on that of Chicago rhythm and blues artists such as Howling Wolf, Muddy Waters and Bo Diddley.

The genesis of the UK R&B scene was in the original Marquee Club in London's Oxford Street, where Alexis Korner's Blues Incorporated played weekly from May 1962 for the next year or so .

Blues Incorporated included Jack Bruce on bass and Ginger Baker on drums, later to comprise two thirds of Cream. A young student, Mick Jagger, occasionally sat in on vocals.

The UK R&B boom gave many American bluesmen a new lease of life professionally. Veteran US stars who toured Britain in the mid-Sixties included Muddy Waters, John Lee Hooker, Howlin' Wolf and Jimmy Reed.

Profile: THE ROLLING STONES

MICK JAGGER
Born: Michael Philip Jagger, 26 July 1943, Dartford, Kent
KEITH RICHARDS
Born: 18 December 1943, Dartford, Kent
BRIAN JONES
Born: Lewis Brian Hopkin-Jones, 28 February 1942, Cheltenham, Gloucestershire
Died: 3 July 1969, Sussex
BILL WYMAN
Born: William Perks, 23 October 1936, London

CHARLIE WATTS
Born: 2 June 1941, London
MICK TAYLOR (replaced Jones 1969)
Born: 17 July 1948, Welwyn Garden City,
Hertfordshire
RON WOOD (replaced Taylor 1976)
Born: 1 June 1947, Hillingdon, Hertfordshire

Chart Debut: Come On [UK#21, 1963]
Major Hits: It's All Over Now, Little Red Rooster [1964], The Last Time, Satisfaction, Get Off Of My Cloud [1965], Paint It Black [1966], Ruby Tuesday [1967], Jumping Jack Flash [1968], Honky Tonk Women [1969], Brown Sugar [1971], Angie [1973], Miss You [1978] **Major Albums:** The Rolling Stones [1964], Out Of Our Heads [1965], Beggars Banquet [1968], Let It Bleed [1969], Sticky Fingers [1971], Exile On Main Street [1972], Goats Head Soup [1973]

Facts'n'Figures: Official RIAA certified sales figures for the Stones albums in the United States reveal that out of 43 albums released during over the 40 years between 1964 and 2004, an incredible 41 received gold discs for selling more than half a million copies. Of these, 26 went platinum when they topped the million mark, 12 achieving multiplatinum sales of several million.

Top score of all for an individual album went to 1971's *Top Rocks 1964-1971* compilation, which sold an amazing 12 million copies in the US.

ROCKCITY: LONDON
Location: South East England on the River Thames.

Musical Milestones: Earliest UK rock'n'roll acts including Tommy Steele and Cliff Richard first appeared in the 2 I's coffe bar in Soho. Early Sixties R&B took off in Soho clubs the Marquee and the Flamingo. The 1967 psychedelic scene centred on UFO club, Tottenham Court Road. The Beatles made their last-ever public appearance on the roof of their Savile Row offices, 1969. Punk exploded in 100 Club and the Roxy in 1976. Historic London gigs have included the Stones in Hyde Park, Live Aid and 2005's Live 8.

Also Famous For: Fashion, theatre, jellied eels, the Proms, conceptual art, trendy restaurants and fast-disappearing pubs.

Biggest Names: Tommy Steele, Cliff Richard, Johnny Kidd, The Rolling Stones, Dave Clarke, The Kinks, The Who, David Bowie, Pink Floyd, Sex Pistols, Dire Straits, Madness, Blur, Prodigy.

Historic Places:
100 Oxford Street, W1. A jazz club since the Fifties, a site of
    seminal punk in the Seventies, still open.
2I's Coffee Bar, Old Compton Street, Soho. The first
    rock'n'roll and skiffle venue, now just a coffee house.
Roundhouse, Chalk Farm Road, NW1. Old railway shed,
    scene of major psychedelic gatherings in the late Sixties
    and early Seventies. Being redeveloped as an art centre.
3 Savile Row, W1. Where the Beatles famously played on the
    roof, the Apple office moved from this address in 1972.
Troubador Cafe, 263-7 Old Brompton Road, SW5. Earls
    Court coffee house where unknown Dylan played in
    1962, also Hendrix, Joni Mitchell. Still open.
EMI Studios, 3 Abbey Road, NW8 where the Beatles made
    most of their records, and outside there's *the* zebra
    crossing.
Hammersmith Odeon, Queen Caroline Street, W6. Former
    cinema, everyone from the Beatles to Bob Dylan has
    played here. Now called the Apollo.

> *"Secretly, I wanted to look like Jimi Hendrix,*
> *but I could never quite pull it off"*
> Bryan Ferry

SOUL

Soul music was a fusion of elements of Black American gospel music and rhythm and blues, the sacred and the secular – hence the name. Its prime architect, long before it acquired a name, was Ray Charles.

Sam Cooke, who came from a gospel background with his group The Soul Stirrers, was the first soul pop star with hits ranging from the chart-topping 'You Send Me' in 1957 to 1965's 'Shake'.

Other soul pioneers who took the Ray Charles small band as an early model were James Brown – who in the Sixties was hailed as "Soul Brother #1" – and Ike and Tina Turner, whose stage show included an all-girl vocal group The Ikettes, based on Charles' Raelettes.

Soul as such really took off in the Sixties with the music coming out of two centres, Motown and Memphis. The Motown (and Tamla) label and studios were based in "Motortown" – Detroit – and released scores of hits by Mary Wells, The Supremes, Smokey Robinson & The Miracles, The Four Tops, Marvin Gaye, Stevie Wonder and many more. Memphis was home to the Stax studios, whose tough brand of Southern Soul was represented by Rufus Thomas, Booker T. & The MGs, Sam & Dave and Wilson Pickett among others, often released on their subsidiary Volt or New York's Atlantic label.

SWEET SOUL ANTHEMS

Year / Artist / Title / US label

1959
Ray Charles *What'd I Say* Atlantic
1961
Ben E King *Stand By Me* Atco
1962
Arthur Alexander *You Better Move* On Dot
1963
Sam Cooke *Bring It On Home To Me* RCA
1963
Miracles *You've Really Got A Hold on Me* Motown
1965
Otis Redding *I've Been Loving You Too Long* Volt
1965
Wilson Pickett *The Midnight Hour* Atlantic
1965
James Brown *I Got You (I Feel Good)* King
1966
Sam & Dave *Soul Man* Stax
1966
Percy Sledge *When A Man Loves A Woman* Atlantic
1966
Stevie Wonder *Uptight (Everything's Alright)* Tamla
1966
Eddie Floyd *Knock On Wood* Stax
1966
Four Tops *Reach Out I'll Be There* Motown
1967
Aretha Franklin *Respect* Atlantic
1968
Marvin Gaye *I Heard It Through The Grapevine* Tamla

ROCKCITY: MEMPHIS

Location: South western tip of Tennessee, where the border meets Mississippi to the south and Arkansas across the Mississippi river to the west.

Musical Milestones: "Father of the Blues" WC Handy wrote classic songs 'Beale Street Blues', 'Memphis Blues' and others in early 20th century. Sam Phillips opened Sun studios (first as Memphis Recording Service) in early Fifties, recording reputed first-ever rock'n'roll record (Jackie Brenston's Rocket 88, 1951) then Elvis Presley in 1954. Stax Records the hub of Southern soul music in the Sixties.

Also Famous For: Al Green's Tabernacle church, Gibson guitars, the National Civil Rights Museum, big burgers and the Memphis Belle.

Biggest Names: Elvis Presley, Jerry Lee Lewis, Johnny Cash, Roy Orbison, Carl Perkins, Rufus Thomas, Booker T. & The MGs, Sam & Dave, Wilson Pickett, The Boxtops.

Historic Places:
Graceland, 3734 Elvis Presley Boulevard. Kitsch or cool, a must for any rock'n'roll fan.
Sun Studio, 706 Union Avenue. Where it all (or much of it) began.
Soulsville, 926 East McLemore Avenue. The old Stax studio, now the Museum of American Soul Music.
WC Handy House Museum. Moved from its original site, now museum dedicated to the "Father of the Blues".
Beale Street. Try to ignore the tourist trappings, this was once *the* centre of Black American music in the South.

According to the studio musicians who backed Otis Redding on his 1968 hit, 'Dock Of The Bay', the whistling which features at the close of the record was made up on the spot when Otis realized he'd forgotten the words that he'd written for the fade-out ending.

SURF MUSIC

Surf music evoked the rolling waves and sunny optimism of teenage California in the early Sixties, with both instrumental and vocal hits contributing to the sound.

Although the Beach Boys are the group most closely associated with the Surf vocal sound, the style originated with the duo Jan & Dean, who had no less than 24 entries in the US Top 100 between 1959 and 1966.

One of Jan and Dean's first records was a song called 'Linda', written in 1944 by Jack Lawrence, about a friend's two year old daughter, Linda Eastman. That same little girl would grow up to marry Paul McCartney in March, 1969.

SURFIN' THE CHARTS – TEN BIGGEST BEACH BUSTERS

US chart peak

1963	Beach Boys	Surfin' USA	3
1963	Chantays	Pipeline	4
1963	Jan & Dean	Surf City	1
1963	Surfaris	Wipe Out	2
1963	Trashmen	Surfin' Bird	4
1963	Marketts	Out Of Limits	3
1954	Beach Boys	Fun, Fun, Fun	5
1964	Jan & Dean	Little Old Lady (From Pasadena)	3
1965	Beach Boys	Help Me Rhonda	1
1965	Beach Boys	California Girls	3

The Beach Boys had the first surf record to make the Top 5 with 'Surfin USA' in April 1963, but were beaten to the top spot by Jan & Dean two months later with 'Surf City' – though the latter was written by Beach Boy Brian Wilson.

The Surf instrumental sound was pioneered by guitarist Dick Dale, followed by hits in the genre that included singles by the Chantays, the Surfaris and the Trashmen.

Dale's unique left-handed guitar technique, playing it upside down instead of re-stringing the instrument, was said to have influenced Jimi Hendrix.

Not to be confused with the British studio group The Tornados whose 'Telstar' hit big in 1962, one of the very first surf instrumentals was 'Bustin' Surfboards', a minor hit for California group The Tornadoes in 1962. To avoid confusion with the UK chart-toppers, the group subsequently changed their name to The Hollywood Tornadoes.

One of the last instrumental surf records to hit the charts, the Marketts 'Out Of Limits' was a surf-style version of the *Outer Limits* TV series theme.

LEGENDARY GIGS

MONTEREY POP FESTIVAL

Two years before Woodstock, over three days 32 acts played to the first great gathering of the "alternative society" of young people, celebrating "music, peace, flower power and love" and heralding the summer of love.

Official Name: The First Annual Monterey International Pop Music Festival

Location: Monterey County Fairgrounds, Monterey, California

Date: June 16, 17 & 18, 1967

Acts: The Association, Beverly, Big Brother & The Holding Company with Janis Joplin, The Blues Project, Booker T. and The MG's with The Mar-Keys, Buffalo Springfield, Eric Burdon & The Animals, Paul Butterfield Blues Band, The Byrds, Canned Heat, Country Joe and The Fish, The Electric Flag, The Grateful Dead, The Group With No Name, Jimi Hendrix Experience, Jefferson Airplane, Al Kooper, Scott McKenzie, The Mamas and The Papas, Hugh Masakela, Steve Miller Band, Moby Grape, Laura Nyro, The Paupers, Quicksilver Messenger Service, Lou Rawls, Otis Redding, Johnny Rivers, Ravi Shankar, Simon and Garfunkel, The Who.

Crowd estimate: 200,000 plus

WOODSTOCK

The most legendary of them all. Over 600,000 people trekked to Max Yasgur's farm site, though many didn't make it. Celebrated – and famously filmed – as the ultimate hippy gathering, it degenerated into a chaotic free concert when the organizers simply couldn't cope as the rains came down. In the mudbath and exodus that ensued, an estimated 320,000 had left before Jimi Hendrix played the final set.

Official Name: Woodstock Music & Art Fair

Location: Max Yasgur's Farm, Bethel, New York

Date: August 15, 16 & 17, 1969

Acts: Joan Baez, The Band, Blood, Sweat & Tears, The Paul Butterfield Blues Band, Canned Heat, Joe Cocker, Country Joe McDonald and The Fish, Creedence Clearwater Revival, Crosby, Stills, & Nash, The Grateful Dead, Arlo Guthrie, Tim Hardin, The Keef Hartley Band, Richie Havens , Jimi Hendrix, Incredible String Band, Jefferson Airplane, Janis Joplin, Melanie, Mountain, Quill, Santana, John Sebastian, Sha-Na-Na, Ravi Shankar, Sly & The Family Stone, Bert Sommer, Sweetwater, Ten Years After, The Who, Johnny Winter, Neil Young.

Crowd estimate: 400,000 – plus another 250,000 who never made it to the site

ISLE OF WIGHT, 1969

The second of three Isle of Wight festivals on consecutive years, this was certainly the most celebrated, mainly because the headline act was the much-awaited appearance of Bob Dylan who had only played once or twice during three years 'retirement' after a motorcycle accident. Dylan closed the second night with just over an hour-long set, in front of the biggest audience for a rock show the UK – or Bob Dylan for that matter – had ever seen.

Official Name: Isle of Wight Festival of Music

Location: Wootton, Isle of Wight

Date: August 29, 30 & 31, 1969

Acts: The Band, Blodwyn Pig, Blonde On Blonde, Bonzo Dog Dooh Dah Band, Edgar Broughton Band, Joe Cocker, Aynsley Dunbar, Bob Dylan, Eclection, Family, Gary Farr, Fat Mattress, Julie Felix, Free, Gypsy, Richie Havens, Marsha Hunt and White Trash, Indo Jazz Fusions, Liverpool Scene, Marsupilami, Mighty Baby, The Moody Blues, The Nice, Tom Paxton, Pentangle, The Pretty Things, Third Ear Band, The Who.

Crowd estimate: 200,000

LIVE AID

A follow-up to 1984's hugely successful Band Aid single 'Do They Know It's Christmas', the marathon concert and telebroadcast was staged to raise money for the starving in Africa. Two concerts were held in London and Philadelphia, broadcast live to an estimated 1.5 billion viewers in 160 countries . By the time the show finished, over $70 million had been raised in telephone pledges worldwide, the figure eventually rising to an incredible $140 million.

Official Name: Live Aid

Location: Wembley Stadium, London & JFK Stadium, Philadelphia

Date: July 13, 1985

Acts [London]: Adam Ant , Boomtown Rats, David Bowie, Phil Collins, Elvis Costello, Kiki Dee, Dire Straits Bryan Ferry, Bob Geldof, Elton John, Howard Jones, Nik Kershaw, Paul McCartney, Alison Moyet, Queen, Sade, Spandau Ballet,

Status Quo, Sting, Style Council, U2, Ultravox, Wham!, The Who, Paul Young.

[Philadelphia]: Bryan Adams, Ashford & Simpson, Joan Baez, Beach Boys, Black Sabbath, The Cars, Eric Clapton, Albert Collins , Phil Collins, Crosby, Stills and Nash, Bo Diddley, Duran Duran, Bob Dylan, The Four Tops, Hall & Oates, The Hooters , Mick Jagger, John Paul Jones, Judas Priest, Eddie Kendricks, Patti LaBelle, Kenny Loggins, Madonna, Pat Metheny, Jimmy Page, Robert Plant, Billy Ocean, Ozzy Osbourne, Teddy Pendergrass, Tom Petty, Power Station, Pretenders, Keith Richards, David Ruffin, Run DMC, Santana, Simple Minds, Speedwagon, Rick Springfield, Tina Turner, Thompson Twins, George Thorogood and the Destroyers, Bernard Watson, Ron Wood.

Plus live video feeds: Autograph (from Russia), INXS (from Australia), B.B. King (from Holland), Udo Lindenberg (from Germany), Loudness (from Japan), Opus (from Austria), Yu Rock Mission (from Serbia)

Crowd estimate: 72,000 in London plus 90,000 in Philadelphia

Television viewing estimate: 1.5 billion

Tommy James and The Shondells turned down an offer to perform at the original Woodstock Festival, after their booking agent described the event as "...a stupid gig on a pig farm in upstate New York".

What was reckoned to be the world's biggest-ever jam session took place at Cheney Stadium, Tacoma, Washington in August 2003, when 754 guitarists played a ten-minute version of 'Louie, Louie'.

TITANIC TOURS

THE BRITISH INVASION

After The Beatles crashed the American charts in the first few months of 1964, they spearheaded what became known as the British Invasion of groups through the next couple of years.

When The Beatles' 'I Want To Hold Your Hand' was released in America in January 1964, it became the fastest selling single in the history of recorded music and Capitol's pressing plant was forced to run 24 hours a day, trying to fill more than a million orders.

Unknown in the US on New Year's Day 1964, The Beatles had the four top singles and the two top albums in the American charts by the end of March, representing 60% of all records sold in the United States.

The names who made it in the US after The Beatles weren't always the most popular – and certainly not the most fashionable – on their home ground. Along with R&B outfits The Animals and The Rolling Stones, UK names who scored Stateside included Herman's Hermits, The Dave Clark Five and Chad & Jeremy, the latter virtually unknown in Great Britain.

As the Brit groups toured the US through 1964, '65 and '66; it took the West Coast bands of the psychedelic era to re-establish American rock on the live concert circuit.

BRITISH HITS IN US TOP TWENTY, 1964 – 1965		
Act	**Hits**	**#1s**
Animals	6	1
Beatles	21	11
Chad & Jeremy	3	–
Dave Clark Five	12	1
Wayne Fontana & The Mindbenders	1	1
Freddie & The Dreamers	4	1
Gerry & The Pacemakers	6	–
Herman's Hermits	7	2
Kinks	5	–
Peter & Gordon	6	1
Rolling Stones	7	2
Searchers	7	–
Zombies	3	–

BOB DYLAN'S NEVER-ENDING TOUR

Bob Dylan has been gigging more or less continuously since 1988, on what has become known as the "never-ending tour". He was at an artistic watershed in his career, and drastically decided to go back on the road with a small band, playing whatever venues took his fancy.

As well as the major cities of the world, Dylan chooses to play in more unusual settings. In America that often means state fairs, corporate events, urban street fairs and even casinos, and in 2005 he undertook his second summer tour of minor-league baseball fields.

Night by night Dylan delves into his enormous repertoire of songs, the musicians often not knowing beforehand what he's going to choose. He'll pick anything from obscure folk ballads to his own timeless classics, to his latest album tracks, to standard pop songs. But even his own best-known items are rendered almost unrecognizable as he re-invents them there on stage.

Playing about a hundred dates a year, since the "tour" began Dylan had clocked up more than 1,700 appearances by mid-2005.

THE STONES KEEP ON ROLLING

It's been a long trek from their first gigs at the Ealing Jazz Club in West London in 1962, but over the 40-plus years since The Rolling Stones' debut their tours have become the biggest earners in the history of rock'n'roll.

The record for the largest grossing rock tour of all time is held by the Stones, after their 1994-95 "Voodoo Lounge" trek took in an amazing $320 million . And second place in that lucrative league is also occupied by the band, the 2002-03 "Forty Licks" tour attracting a total audience of over 3.4 million people and bringing in $300 million.

The Stones 2005 show at the Hollywood Bowl broke all records as the most expensive rock concert ever. 18,000 tickets for the Novemmber date were snapped up online in minutes, even though the top price was over $400 dollars a seat.

A comparative calculation made in the London *Sunday Times* revealed that the Hollywood Bowl concert would cost fans up to £2 ($3.5) per minute to watch Mick and the boys, compared with 91 pence ($1.5) a minute for Paul McCartney's US 2005 tour and a paltry 32 pence (55 cents) to see Destiny's Child.

Even though they don't make as much from records as they used to, the Stones have earned £1.23 billion (over $2 billion) in the past 16 years largely from live concert revenue and the associated merchandising

ROCK'N'ROLL PEOPLE

═══ BIRTHS'N'DEATHS ═══

Famous Birthplaces

Some towns and cities are celebrated for a million reasons, others are just names on the map that you might never think about twice were it not for their status in the rock history books as famous birthplaces.

Albany, Georgia	Ray Charles
Dartford, Kent	Mick Jagger
Duluth, Minnesota	Bob Dylan
Ferriday, Louisiana	Jerry Lee Lewis
Freehold, New Jersey	Bruce Springsteen
Highland Park, Michigan	Bill Haley
Kingsland, Arkansas	Johnny Cash
Lubbock, Texas	Buddy Holly
Macon, Georgia	Little Richard, James Brown
McComb, Mississippi	Bo Diddley
Madison, Wisconsin	Otis Redding
Melbourne, Florida	Jim Morrison
Port Arthur, Texas	Janis Joplin
Pratville, Alabama	Wilson Pickett
Ripley, Surrey	Eric Clapton
Saginaw, Michigan	Stevie Wonder
San Jose, California	Chuck Berry
Tiptonville, Tennessee	Carl Perkins
Tupelo, Mississippi	Elvis Presley
Vernon, Texas	Roy Orbison

═══ WHAT'S IN A NAME? ═══

We've all read how The Beatles were once called Johnny & The Moondogs, and The Who, The High Numbers. More obscurely, it's less well known that, trying to jump on the British beat bandwagon, The Byrds originally called themselves The Beefeaters. And that, barely out of high school, Simon and Garfunkel put themselves round as Tom & Jerry. Not as barmy as Simple Minds however, who somehow thought that Johnny & The Self Abusers would catch on.

Long-winded names were often a recipe for confusion. One dance hall promoter in the North of England, who knew little about the new-fangled beat groups he was booking into his venue, billed Long John Baldry & The Hoochie Coochie Men as "Big Jack Bradley & The Hokey Cokey Men"!

But prize for the most imaginative name goes to a Seventies band hailing from Runcorn in the UK North West – Ward Robe & The Tall Boys, featuring lead singer Chester Drawers.

TEN NAME CHANGES THAT WORKED

Born	Became
Anna Mae Bullock	Tina Turner
Eric Clapp	Eric Clapton
Reg Dwight	Elton John
Ernest Evans	Chubby Checker
Vincent Furnier	Alice Cooper
Steveland Morris Hardaway	Stevie Wonder
Otha Ellas Bates McDaniel	Bo Diddley
McKinley Morganfield	Muddy Waters
James Jewel Osterberg	Iggy Pop
Don Van Vliet	Captain Beefheart

CAR CRASH BLUES AND OTHER SUDDEN DEATHS

Date / Artist / Location / Cause

3 February 1959 **Buddy Holly** Mason City, Iowa
Air crash which also took the lives of
Richie Valens and the Big Bopper

17 April 1960 **Eddie Cochran** Bath, UK
Car crash which also injured fellow rocker Gene Vincent

11 December 1964 **Sam Cooke** Los Angeles
Murdered, shot by motel manageress

10 December 1967 **Otis Redding** Madison, Wisconsin
Air crash, also killed were four of his backing group
the Bar-Kays

16 September 1977 **Marc Bolan** London
Car crash

7 January 1980 **Larry Williams** Los Angeles
Suicide

8 December 1980 **John Lennon** New York City
Murdered; shot by fan Mark Chapman

1 April 1984 **Marvin Gaye** Los Angeles
Murdered, shot by his father

5 April 1994 **Kurt Cobain** Seattle
Suicide

22 November 1997 **Michael Hutchence**
Sydney, Australia Suicide

THE WORLD'S
LOUDEST

Back in 1964, an acoustics expert from New South Wales University measured the noise level during a Beatles' concert at 112 decibels. That's between 10 and 20 decibels higher than a Boeing 707 jet flying at 2,000 feet. This was long before the days of marathon amplification – the Beatles played through what would now be considred very modest equipment – so one can only assume that most of the excrutiating volume was produced by screaming fans!

Deep Purple held the title of "World's Loudest Rock Band" in the 1975 *Guiness Book of World Records*, but it only lasted for a year. In 1976 The Who entered the book as the loudest ever, when they reached 120 decibels during a show at the Charlton Athletic football ground in England

Heavy metal veterans Motorhead held the title for a five-year run before being eventually outgunned by AC/DC.

Though not setting any records, during a concert in Rome in 1992, U2 set off earthquake alarms in two neighboorhoods.

Metal monsters Manowar, meanwhile, set the record at an ear-splitting 129.5 decibels during a tour of Britain in 1984. Through their ten tons of amplifiers and speakers the band even managed to crank it up past this when they were playing in Germany in 1994, bassist Joey DeMaio registering an awsome 130.7 – just ten less decibels than a Boeing 747 produces on take-off.

ROCK OF AGES

The Rolling Stones are one of the longest-serving rock groups on the planet, now well into their fifth decade having been formed in 1963. And as The Spectres, Brit rockers Status Quo first got together as an instrumental group a year earlier, in 1962, and are still going strong. But the American group The Ventures top that; still touring, they originally got together in 1959, enjoying their first chart entry in 1960.

And some of rock's true veterans are still on the road. While Fats Domino (born 1928) takes it easy, playing at special events like the annual New Orleans Jazz and Heritage Festival, Chuck Berry (born 1926), Little Richard (1932) and Jerry Lee Lewis (1935) tread the boards worldwide, including a 'Legends Of Rock'n'Roll' European trek which they made in the summer of 2005. At 79, Berry makes young Jagger look a mere slip of a lad.

CULT FIGURES

JOHNNY ACE

The wonderfully-named Ace (actually John Marshall Alexander) was guaranteed cult status after shooting himself dead while playing Russian roulette in a Houston dressing room on Christmas Eve 1954. He'd played with the seminal Memphis outfit the Beale Streeters in the late Forties, whose line-up included bluesmen BB King and Bobby Bland, and had a #1 single in the R&B charts with his first solo effort 'My Song'. His mellow baritone voice graced another six entries in the R&B Top Ten, the posthumous 'Pledging My Love' topping the list and making the pop Top Twenty in 1955. Paul Simon sang 'The Late Great Johnny Ace' in 1983, comparing the singer's death to that of John Lennon.

THE FUGS

The earliest of New York's underground groups, the Fugs were formed by beat generation poets Tuli Kupferberg and Ed Sanders in 1964, who performed (with drummer Ken Weaver and various backing musicians) an outrageous repertoire of pro-drugs songs, humorous obscenity and vigorous ant-war propaganda. With the albums *First Album, The Fugs (Kill For Peace)* and *Virgin Fugs* they pre-dated the alternative society of the hippy movement, and went on to provide peace protesters with a rallying chant in 'Exorcising The Evil Spirits From The Pentagon' on their 1968 album *Tenderness Junction*.

WANDA JACKSON

Had the music not been such a male preserve in its early days, Wanda Jackson could have easily been the First Lady of rock'n'roll – or more accurately, rockabilly. Starting out as a country ballad singer, after a 1955 stint supporting Elvis on tour she developed a wild style which got her signed to Capitol Records, who felt she could be the female answer to their star rocker Gene Vincent. She made some extraordinary records including 'Hot Dog! That Made Him Mad' in 1956, 'Fujiyama Mama' (1958) and an explosively raunchy cover of Elvis' 'Let's Have A Party' in 1960. The fact she held her own on tours with Elvis, Jerry Lee and Carl Perkins attested to her tough talent, but she was way ahead of her time. By the early Sixties she'd settled into the more predictable role model of a sentimental country singer, and later went on to specialize in gospel recordings.

THE RISING SONS

A cult name even in their own time, the Rising Sons were formed in 1964 when teenage guitarists Taj Mahal and Jesse Lee Kincaid drove from Cambridge, Massachusetts to form a band in Los Angeles. There, Kincaid knew 17-year old Ryland Cooder, and the two sought out the already brilliant guitarist who was "smoking cigars and driving a maroon '47 Packard

four-door saloon with a straight-8 and whitewalls" according
to Taj. With Gavin Marker on bass and Kevin Kelley on drums
they became The Rising Sons, and immitaely became a hit
on the LA club scene. With musical ambitions that met
somewhere between Beatles-inspired pop and hardcore
rhythm and blues, they only ever released one single – Skip
James' 'The Devils Got My Woman' and 'Candy Man' written
by Reverend Gary Davis. – but cut more than enough tracks
for an album, 22 in all. Produced by the Byrds' Terry Melcher,
the music crackles with enthusiasm and precocious
technique. Taj Mahal and Ry Cooder both went on to be big
names of course, Cooder in particular as a sidman to Captain
Beefheart, a bandleader in his own right, and a pioneer in the
promotion of "world music" via projects like the Buena Vista
Social Club.

SOME OTHER CULT NAMES WORTH TRACKING DOWN

Ella Mae Morse: White boogie-R&B singer who hit the big
time through the Forties and early Fifties. **Key Recording:**
'House Of Blue Lights', 1946

Dell-Vikings: One of the first racially integrated doo-wop
groups, and hugely influential. **Key Recording:** 'Come Go
With Me', 1957

Link Wray: Influential guitarist who invented the fuzz-tone
by punching a hole in an amp speaker with a pencil. **Key
Recording:** 'Rumble', 1958

Johnny Kidd & The Pirates: Widely regarded as the most
important UK rocker before The Beatles. **Key Recording:**
'Shakin' All Over', 1960.

Duffy Power: A sensational British rhythm and blues singer
who never quite made it. **Key Recording:** 'I Saw Her
Standing There', 1963.

Chocolate Watch Band: Archetypal early psychedelic garage band from San Francisco. **Key Recording:** 'Let's Talk About Girls', 1967

WHAT EVER HAPPENED TO...?

Pat Boone:

After famously covering early rock'n'roll classics in the Fifties, and making them even bigger hits as a consequence, Pat Boone confirmed his clean-cut image (white sneakers were his trademark) when he turned to religious evangelism in the Seventies, for a time only making gospel records. He shocked many in 1997, however, when he appeared at the American Music Awards dressed in chains and a leather vest and sporting fake tattoos. He was promoting an album of covers of heavy metal music – entitled *No More Mr Nice Guy* – done in the same anodyne style that had worked for him in the Fifties.

Joey Dee & The Starlighters:

House band at the famed Peppermint Lounge in New York where the Twist craze took off in the early Sixties, Joey Dee & The Starlighters topped the US charts with 'Peppermint Twist' in 1961, and followed through with a couple of more hits. Dee continues to tour on the 'nostalgia' circuit, but the fate of other band members is arguably of more interest. Actor Joe Pesci was a member of the touring Starlighters, playing guitar, and The Ronettes were the backing vocalists and dancers for the club act before being discovered by Phil Spector. Three of the four original Young Rascals were in the band, and in 1964 the guitarist was Jimmy James – also known as Maurice James before he made it big in England as Jimi Hendrix!

Lee Dorsey

Famous for a string of soul dance hits such as 'Working In The Coal Mine, 'Ride Your Pony' and 'Get Out Of My Life Woman' in the mid-Sixties, Dorsey gave up singing regularly to concentrate on his panel-beating company in New Orleans. He came out of retirement to support The Clash on a 1980 US tour, and died in 1986 from emphysema.

Jan & Dean:

After Jan Berry of surf duo Jan & Dean was seriously injured in a car accident in April 1966 and could no longer perform, partner Dean Torrence went into graphic design. He designed over 200 album covers including *The Turtles Golden Hits*, nine for The Nitty Gritty Dirt Band and several for Harry Nilsson. He won a Grammy Award for "Best Album Cover of the Year" in 1972 for the LP *Pollution* by the group of the same name.

Johnnie Ray:

One of the true precursors of rock'n'roll, Ray's on-stage histrionics earned him various nicknames such as "the Cry Guy", "the Nabob of Sob" and "the Prince of Wails". His hits included 1951's 'Cry' and a cover of The Drifter's 'Such A Night' (1954), which although banned for suggestiveness in the US made #1 in the UK. More mainstream hits followed, but in the wake of Elvis' success he failed to maintain his earlier fan following, and after a career resigned to the international cabaret circuit he died of liver failure at the age of 63, brought on by lifelong alcoholism.

Edwin Starr:

Motown singer Edwin Starr enjoyed four US chart hits including a #1, 'War', in 1971. He relocated to the UK where he settled in the small town Midlands of Tamworth, Staffordshire. He was still gigging and making the occasional TV appearance until dying of heart failure in 2003.

BIBLIOGRAPHY AND SOURCES

Beatles *The Beatles Anthology* [Cassell & Co, UK 2000]

Betrock, Allan: *Girl Groups* [Delilah, US 1992]

Betts, Graham: *Complete UK Hit Singles* [Harper Collins, UK 2004]

Brown, Tony: *Complete Book of British Charts* [Omnibus, UK 2000]

Clarke, Donald [ed]: *Penguin Encyclopedia of Popular Music* [Viking, UK 1989]

Cohn, Nik: *Pop From The Beginning* [Weidenfeld & Nicholson, UK 1969]

Ertegun, Ahmet: *What'd I Say: The Atlantic Story* [Orion, UK 2001]

Evans, Mike: *NYC Rock* [Sanctuary, UK 2003]

George, Nelson: *Where Did Our Love Go?. The Rise and Fall of the Motown Sound*
    [Omnibus, UK 1986]

Gillett, Charlie: *The Sound of the City* [Pantheon Books, US 1970]

Gregory, Hugh: *A Century of Pop* [Hamlyn, UK 1998]

Grundy, Stuart & Tobler, John: *The Record Producers* [BBC Books, UK 1982]

Guralnick, Peter *Last Train To Memphis: The Rise of Elvis Presley* [Abacus. UK 1995]

Guralnick, Peter: *Sweet Soul Music* [Virgin Books, UK 1986]

Hardy, Phil: *The Faber Companion to 20th Century Popular Music* [Faber, UK 2001]

Millar, Bill: *The Drifters: The Rise and Fall of the Black Vocal Group* [Studio Vista,
    UK 1971]

Shaw, Arnold: *Black Popular Music in America* [Schirmer, US 1986]

Simpson, Paul [ed]: *The Rough Guide to Cult Pop* [Rough Guides, UK 2003]

Tosches, Nick: *Unsung Heroes of Rock'n'Roll* [Secker & Warburg, VK 1991]

Unterberger, Richie: *Unknown Legends of Rock'n'Roll* [Miller Freeman, US 1998]

Whitburn, Joel: *Billboard Book of USA Top 40 Hits* [Guiness, UK 1989]

Whitburn, Joel: *Billboard Book of Top 40 Albums* [Omnibus, UK 1991]

Wyman, Bill: *Bill Wyman's Blues Odyssey* [Dorling Kindersley, UK 2001]

Wyman, Bill: *Rolling With The Stones* [Dorling Kindersley, UK 2002]

Newspapers and Magazines:
Billboard, the Guardian, Melody Maker, Mersey Beat, Mojo, New Musical Express,
Rolling Stone, Sunday Times

Websites
amazon.com bbc.com
classicrecords.com
msnbc.msn.com
Reuters/Billboard/entertainment-news.org
triumphpc.com/mersey-beat